THE TOMB OF ST. PETER

THE TOMB OF
ST. PETER

THE NEW DISCOVERIES IN THE SACRED
GROTTOES OF THE VATICAN

BY

Margherita Guarducci

WITH AN INTRODUCTION BY

H. V. Morton

TRANSLATED FROM THE ITALIAN BY

Joseph McLellan

GEORGE G. HARRAP & CO. LTD
(LONDON TORONTO WELLINGTON SYDNEY)

This book was originally published in Italy under the title of *La Tomba di Pietro*.

All the photographs and drawings are reproduced through the courtesy of Editrice Studium, Rome, with the exception of Figure 23, courtesy of Edizione Alinari, Rome.

First published in Great Britain 1960
by GEORGE G. HARRAP & CO. LTD
182 High Holborn, London, W.C. 1

© *Editrice Studium* 1959
© *English Translation George G. Harrap & Co. Ltd* 1960

Printed in U.S.A.

INTRODUCTION

PROFESSOR MARGHERITA GUARDUCCI is a distinguished Italian archaeologist whose impressive scientific works upon the epigraphy of the excavations beneath St. Peter's in Rome have created wide interest and comment. This book, of a popular character, places the reader in possession of all that concerns the coming of St. Peter to Rome, his martyrdom, and his burial in the Vatican. Several pages also (chapter V) give the conclusions of the author's epigraphical studies, in which she demonstrated that before St. Peter's was built, Christians sought out the Apostle's tomb in the Vatican Cemetery and covered neighboring walls with prayers, invocations and names.

On one of these walls (Wall G) Professor Guarducci has discovered a religious "cryptography" by which the faithful offered prayers for the eternal life of their dead and, at the same time, expressed their firm Christian faith. Her argument is illustrated by many photographs of the actual inscriptions.

To the general reader, perhaps the most interesting portion of this book will be the author's scholarly account of the

5

pre-Christian and the post-Christian history of that portion
of the Vatican Hill upon which St. Peter's stands, and her
description of the scientific investigation of the space beneath
the high altar, the traditional burial place of St. Peter, which
was undertaken with the authority of the late Pope, Pius
XII. Professor Guarducci notes the disinclination to explore
this site felt by all former ages. "An irresistible prudence, almost an unconquered fear, prevented a thorough investigation of the terrain," she writes. "The fear of finding something down there which would contradict or modify the tradition dear to the faithful overcame the desire to appease a
burning curiosity."

The satisfaction of this "burning curiosity" has, it is true,
modified the popular conception of the Apostle's tomb, but
it has not contradicted the tradition.

A visit to the street of tombs in the ancient Roman cemetery upon which St. Peter's is built (it is thirty feet beneath
the nave and the high altar), is the most impressive and memorable experience that can fall to the lot of anyone in Rome.
The excavations are not open to the public, and entry will
always be restricted to small groups of scholars, historians
and archaeologists.

The visitor descends a flight of steps at the Arco delle
Campane entrance (on the extreme left as you face St.
Peter's) and these lead beneath the Vatican Grottoes into a
dusty silent Roman street which might be in Herculaneum
or Pompeii. Sombre and dignified brick doorways, standing
on each side of the road, afford entry into painted tomb-
chambers where the dead still lie in sarcophagi or in urn
burials. This cemetery, which was used by both pagans and
Christians, was once open to the sun and air, but has known
no daylight since Constantine the Great built the basilica
upon it sixteen centuries ago. Now, by the stark light of un-
shaded electric bulbs, and beneath a roof of iron and steel,

the visitor explores this street, reading the names of those buried there so long ago, until he comes to that space below the high altar which archaeologists can recognize as the tomb, or the memorial, of St. Peter. To the layman, it is a scene of some confusion where walls of different dates, and marble coffins embedded in masonry, are crowded together side by side, and only the trained eye can detect the essential pattern. The visitor can only reflect with awe that he is standing in a place venerated by Christians since the first century. The visible evidence of such veneration is the theme of this fascinating book.

—H. V. MORTON

PREFACE

ABOUT 333 A.D., in his work entitled *Theophania,* the Christian historian Eusebius, Bishop of Caesarea, wrote of Peter: ". . . he was known throughout the world, even in the Western countries, and his memory, among the Romans, is still more alive than the memory of all those who lived before him; so much so that he is honored with a splendid tomb overlooking the city. To this tomb, countless crowds come from all parts of the Roman Empire, as to a great sanctuary and temple of God."[1]

In 333, indeed, there was already a monument on the Vatican Hill, built almost twenty years earlier by the Emperor Constantine to enclose the little chapel over the Apostle's tomb. Above the monument rose—although it had not yet been finished—the basilica in which the same emperor had decided to glorify the first vicar of Christ (Fig. 1).

Today the basilica of Constantine has disappeared. The taste of the Renaissance, avid for classic lines and grandiose forms, chose to tear it down and to substitute another, equally notable building—the splendid church by Bramante crowned with the lofty dome by Michelangelo. On this new

9

basilica each passing century has left its mark. The seventeenth and eighteenth centuries lavished glorious ornaments on it; the nineteenth century created noble works inspired by nostalgic love of ancient art; and our own century has accomplished, and continues to undertake, notable works of restoration and decoration.

But if the course of centuries and innumerable changes have radically transformed the appearance of the basilica, the words of Eusebius remain—we might say—up to date. Christians still come to the shrine of Peter and linger there in prayer. They come from all parts of the world; from near and far, often from very far (the modern world is so much larger than that known to Eusebius!); they come by land, sea and air. They come dressed in the most varied fashions, speaking many foreign languages.

What are the thoughts that stir in their hearts? Probably they might run like this: "Peter is the Galilean fisherman whom Christ chose among the disciples to be His vicar on earth; Peter came to Rome to preach the Gospel; there he died, a martyr, crucified like his Master, during the persecution of Nero, and he was buried on the Vatican Hill. Above his tomb rises the greatest church in Christendom; nearby the Pontiff, successor to Peter and custodian of divine truth, has his See. The tomb of the Apostle is therefore the solid rock on which the Church is founded; it is the symbol of its unity and of its strength against the forces of evil; it is a consolation for the faithful aspiring to the heavenly kingdom, for which Peter, through the will of Christ, holds the keys."

The thoughts of the Christians who crowd reverently into the Basilica of St. Peter agree with the age-old tradition of the Church.

But this serene and certain faith has not been shared by all in the past and is not universally held today. Men have tried many times, and they are still trying, to strike the Roman tradition at its root, denying the martyrdom and even the presence of Peter in Rome.

The first attacks were launched in the thirteenth century, at the height of the Middle Ages, by the Waldensian sect. Stubbornly maintaining that it was necessary to reject any traditions not found in the Bible, they denied the tradition of St. Peter's journey to Rome and his martyrdom there. We shall see in later pages that this judgment is incorrect, since Holy Scripture offers us, in the first Epistle of St. Peter himself, a very significant clue supporting the Roman tradition. But the seeds of doubt planted by the Waldensians bore their fruit; not immediately, but—as happens often in history —in later centuries.

Luther and the first adherents of the Reformation did not show any special interest in the questions of the presence or martyrdom of Peter in Rome. As for the tombs of the two Apostles, Peter and Paul, they merely affirmed that nothing was certain concerning them. It is sufficient to mention, on this point, the words written by Luther in 1545, in the book entitled *Against the Roman Papacy Instituted by the Devil:* "I am content to be able to say, since I have seen it and heard it at Rome, that it is unknown where in the city the bodies of Saint Peter and Saint Paul are located, or even whether they are there at all. Even the Pope and the cardinals know very well that they do not know."[2]

We cannot be sure from what source in Rome Luther obtained this information, but there is clearly some exaggeration involved, for in the sixteenth century the great majority of Romans accepted without question the common and very old tradition that the remains of the two Apostles lay within the two basilicas located, respectively, in the Vatican and on the Via Ostiense.

In the seventeenth century and, again, in the nineteenth,

Protestant attacks on the Roman tradition became more violent, and they continue today. The chief contemporary representative of this tendency is Karl Heussi, who has published more than ten writings of varied importance to prove that St. Peter never came to Rome and cannot be buried there. Heussi's most recent work, entitled *A Critical Look at the Roman Tradition of Peter*,[3] was published in 1955.

But it cannot be said that all Protestant scholars have united against the Roman tradition. Some, indeed, have welcomed it rather liberally and strenuously defended it. It is sufficient to mention the well-known names of Adolph von Harnack, John Lietzmann, and Oscar Cullman. Lietzmann, who died in 1942, succeeded in refuting some of Heussi's writings in his time,[4] while more recently another German scholar, Konrad Aland, has answered Heussi's later writings.

At this point it is appropriate to ask: Who is right? Can the Roman tradition really be accepted? And if it cannot be accepted entirely, can part of it be accepted?[5]

To answer these questions, which have occurred to many truth-seeking minds, there is only one method: to examine calmly the documents, that is—in this case—the literary sources and the results of archaeological investigations.

The ancient writers have given us important information on the martyrdom and the burial of Peter. The researches and the excavations undertaken up to now in the Vatican region, and particularly under and around the basilica, have added the weight of their testimony to this ancient information. There are also the excavations completed under and around the Church of St. Sebastian on the Appian Way, and we must consider these to decide whether it is possible—as some maintain—that the remains of St. Peter were kept for some time, with those of St. Paul, in that location.

In writing these pages, I propose to summarize what is known for certain and to clarify as much as possible what is obscure, seeking to combine the most scrupulous scientific accuracy with simplicity of exposition. This is particularly necessary since my words are directed specially to those who, without being historians or archaeologists or professional scholars, wish to have precise information on this problem which has aroused and continues to arouse such intense and widespread interest.

—THE AUTHOR

CONTENTS

15

ILLUSTRATIONS

PLATES

* In the Italian text "G" is shown as a lower case letter. Ed.

THE TOMB OF ST. PETER

I

~

THE TESTIMONY OF
ANCIENT AUTHORS

ROME WAS THE SITE OF PETER'S MARTYRDOM. This is the statement repeated unanimously by many ancient authors; no author, we might add, asserts that he suffered martyrdom anywhere else. It is easy to see that this very eloquently supports the Roman tradition. Indeed, if this tradition had not had very solid foundations, it is probable that some voice would have been raised to point out in another city the place where Peter gave, through martyrdom, the supreme testimony to the Faith. Opportunities certainly would not have been overlooked. In the second century, for example, the Christian communities of Ephesus and other places in Asia Minor, which had begun to show feelings of rivalry toward the Church of Rome, would have been quite happy if they had been able to deny Rome's boast of having within its walls the tomb of the first vicar of Christ. But no one, so far as we can determine, ever attempted—then or later—to dispute this distinction claimed by Rome.

So far as St. Peter's journey to Rome and his stay there are concerned, we must admit that in the Epistles of St. Paul, no explicit indications can be found. Indeed, in the famous Epistle to the Romans, written between 57 and 58 A.D., Paul does not mention the name of Peter among those to whom he sends greetings. Similarly, in the two Epistles which he wrote from Rome, to the Collosians (between 60 and 62 A.D.?) and to Timothy (in 62 or shortly thereafter), Peter is not named among those who, through Paul, send their greetings to distant brethren. Some scholars have attempted to deduce from this that, at least on these three occasions, Peter was not in Rome. This is possible; on the other hand, we cannot completely exclude the possibility that Peter's name was omitted on purpose for reasons of prudence or for other motives unknown to us. In addition, it is not improbable that when St. Paul, in the Epistle to the Romans,[1] refers to the work of Christian evangelism already undertaken in Rome "by others" he had St. Peter in mind. Certainly it is hard to believe that Peter, who had taken upon himself the task of preaching to the Jews, would have neglected to go very promptly to Rome, where there was, at that time, a very large Jewish colony.

Nor is explicit mention of Peter's journey to Rome found in the Acts of the Apostles. But we must consider that the Acts end abruptly with the arrival of Paul in Rome and that the martyrdom of the two Apostles falls outside the scope of the work, at least in the form in which it has come down to us.

On the other hand, there is very clear testimony of Peter's stay in Rome in the first Epistle—certainly authentic—of Peter himself. At the end of this Epistle, written, apparently, in the year 64 to the Christian communities of Asia Minor, the Apostle sends the following words to the distant faithful: "The community of the elect in Babylon sends you greetings; so does my son, Mark."[2] Mark is usually identified with the

Evangelist as Peter's spiritual son; and Babylon is without doubt the place from which the Apostle is writing. But which Babylon is it? It would be absurd to think of the Babylon in Mesopotamia, since no mention has come down to us of a journey by Peter into that remote region; and in addition it is known that the Mesopotamian Babylon was practically abandoned by the Jews about the middle of the first century.[3] It would be even more far-fetched to identify Peter's Babylon with an obscure Babylon in Egypt, mentioned by the geographer Strabo and by others as a military outpost.[4] The Protestant scholar Karl Heussi, who denies with such energy that Peter ever visited Rome, finds in the Babylon of the Petrine Epistle a metaphorical concept more or less equivalent to that of the word *Diaspora* found at the beginning of the Epistle. In other words, Babylon would be the whole group of "faithful without a homeland" who aspire to the better life promised by Christ. But the use of "Babylon" in this sense is not attested in any document, and besides it is quite clear that the Apostle refers here to a true and particular city.

Now, it is a well-known fact that in the first centuries of the Christian era there was a widespread custom of applying the name of Babylon to Rome. This custom was part of a massive movement of hostility toward Rome, a movement which had originated and continued to receive its principal momentum from the Jewish community.[5] The radical difference between the Roman mentality and that of the Jews had aroused in the latter a dull resentment which later, after the destruction of Jerusalem by order of the Emperor Titus in the year 70, became an implacable hatred. In harmony with this attitude, the Jews had given Rome the name of Babylon, which assumed, for them, a profound significance. Babylon was the city through whose crime the Jews had suffered so much, just as they were suffering now through the crimes of

FIG. 1. Interior of Constantine's fourth century basilica, from a seventeenth century fresco in the Vatican Grottoes.

Rome; Babylon was the wicked, corrupt city, as wicked and corrupt as Rome, in that era, appeared to them; Babylon had been destroyed, becoming almost a symbol of human power crumbled to dust, and they wished exactly the same fate to fall on Rome.

Therefore it is not strange that Peter, without giving the name "Babylon" an accent of hatred, still followed a usage long very common among the Jews and among Orientals in general. This interpretation has been 'adopted by many Christian authors, some of them quite ancient. Now if "Babylon" is equivalent to "Rome," it follows that Peter dictated his first Epistle at Rome, foreseeing the terrible tests that he himself and his flock would have to face and trying to stir up in their souls their faith in the promises of Christ.

On the fact of Peter's martyrdom, we have certain information. In St. John's Gospel, written, apparently, near the end of the first century, is found the phrase spoken by Christ to Peter, after exhorting him to feed His sheep:[6] "Amen, amen

I say unto you, when you were younger you would gird your-self and walk where you wished to go; but when you have grown old you will stretch out your hands and another will gird you and take you where you do not wish to go." And St. John adds: "He told him this to show the death with which he would glorify God. And when He had said this, He told him, 'Follow me.' "

The expression "stretch out the hands," common in the time of St. John, had the special meaning of "die on the cross." In addition, the invitation "Follow me," which Christ gave to Peter after predicting his martyrdom, is quite signifi-cant. Christ seems to mean that Peter must follow Him even in his manner of death; dying, like the Master, on the cross.

Another clear indication of the Apostle's martyrdom is found in Peter's second Epistle, in the words: "knowing that soon I must leave my mortal body, as Our Lord Jesus Christ revealed to me."[7] The authenticity of this Epistle is not uni-versally recognized; but even those who deny it admit that it is a very ancient text, difficult to date after about 150 A.D.

The above-mentioned sections of the New Testament clearly refer to the martyrdom of Peter, without indicating precisely where it took place; but there are other documents from which it is apparent that it happened in Rome.

On this point, many scholars have quoted two famous passages: one, taken from the first Epistle to the Corinthians of St. Clement of Rome; the other, from the Epistle to the Romans of St. Ignatius of Antioch. St. Clement was Bishop of Rome at the end of the first and the beginning of the second century (approximately 92-101 A.D.). This is a time so close to that in which the Apostles Peter and Paul preached and died that he may have known them personally. In addition, he was a native of Rome and, as a Roman, must have been better informed than others on things that had happened in the City. He seems to have written the first Epistle to the Corinthians in the year 96, when the faithful in Rome had hardly finished with the fierce persecutions by the Emperor Domitian, and the memory of these dramatic events must have been very strong in the mind of St. Clement. The purpose of the Epistle was to smooth out the discords which had appeared among the Christians of Corinth and which, if they were not quickly subdued, might have brought on very serious evils. To achieve his purpose, St. Clement tries to put the Corinthians on guard against jealousy, envy and discord, showing them with ancient and contemporary examples that these fatal passions bring death to families and to society. After speaking of Cain and Abel, of Esau and Jacob and other famous names from the Old Testament, he comes to the eloquent and terrifying cases of his own generation and recalls in particular those heroes of the Church (he calls them "pillars") who were persecuted and killed because of jealousy and envy. "Let us consider," he writes, "our good Apostles, Peter and Paul, who suffered not one but many trials through unjust jealousy, and thus, having given testimony, went to the deserved place of glory. Because of jealousy and discord, Paul bore the palm of suffering . . . and having given his testimony before the rulers, left the world and was taken up to the holy place."

Saint Clement then records that, together with the Apostles, "a great number of the elect" suffered because of jealousy, that they had to endure many outrages and tortures; that there were heroic women among them who "having suffered terrible and impious mistreatments, took the sure road of the Faith and obtained a glorious reward."[8]

Without doubt, St. Clement was referring to the victims of the persecution of Nero. This is clearly demonstrated by consulting a famous passage in the *Annals* of Tacitus,[9] where the great Roman historian recalls the tragic events of the burning of Rome (July 19, 64 A.D.) and of the persecution launched by Nero against the Christians to place on them the blame for the fire that he himself had arranged. Tacitus speaks of the great number of the faithful whom Nero had imprisoned and killed with the most cruel tortures, during horrible spectacles staged in the Vatican gardens and particularly in the arena. Some of the words he uses correspond exactly to the Greek words in the Epistle of St. Clement. Now, if St. Clement associates the memory of Peter and Paul with that of the victims of Nero's persecution, this means, in all probability, that the Apostles were victims of the same persecution. The fact of their martyrdom is confirmed by other particulars in St. Clement's text. Thus, the Greek verb μαρτυρεῖν (*martyrein*) used by St. Clement to indicate the "testimony" which they gave to Christ, signifies usually, in Christian texts, testimony given with blood, i.e., with martyrdom. Two other expressions, "place of glory" (τόπος τῆς δόξης— *topos tes doxes*) and "holy place" (ἅγιος τόπος— *hagios topos*) used by St. Clement to indicate the place where the Apostles received the reward of their heroic virtue, refer perfectly to those who have sealed with martyrdom their faith in Christ. It is also very significant that St. Clement repeatedly deplores the jealousy and envy found among followers of the same Christian religion. This insistence recalls to our memory the sorrowful words with which St. Paul refers to "false brethren"[10] and condemns "jealousy" and "discord" among Christians who preach the same Gospel.[11] There is also confirmation from Tacitus who, in the famous passage on Nero's persecution tells us precisely that the great number of Christians killed in this persecution were captured as a result of denunciations by a few who had been arrested first. All these indications concur to show that St. Clement considered Peter and Paul the most outstanding martyrs of Nero's persecution, drawn to death by the jealousy and discord of their own brethren.

The other passage usually cited by scholars to prove the

FIG. 2. St. Peter placed under arrest. Detail from a sarcophagus datable about 325 A.D. (from the excavations under St. Peter's). The monogram of Christ (☧) can be seen on the scroll of the law which Peter holds in his hand.

martyrdom of Peter in Rome is, as I have mentioned, that of St. Ignatius of Antioch in his Epistle to the Romans. During the reign of the Emperor Trajan, and precisely, it would seem, in 107, Ignatius, Bishop of Antioch in Syria, had been condemned to a horrible death: to be exposed to wild animals in the arena, *ad bestias,* in the language of the time. Imprisoned in Antioch, St. Ignatius was sent with other Christians to Rome where his martyrdom was to take place. Sustained by a marvelous faith, he went through the stages of the long and painful journey by land and sea, yearning with tremulous joy for the suffering from which he would rise to the glory of heaven. During the trip there was a delay at Smyrna, and the heroic bishop took advantage of it to dictate several letters. Among others, he dictated one directly to the Christians of Rome, the city in which he knew he would soon lose his earthly life. In this Epistle, he exhorts the Romans not to make any attempt to rescue him; rather they should pray to Christ that his body might disappear completely—a total holocaust—in the jaws of the beasts. And just at this point, Ignatius finds it necessary to add: "I do not command you as did Peter and Paul; they were Apostles and I am a condemned man, they were free men and I, until now, a slave. But if I suffer martyrdom, I shall be a freeman of Jesus and I shall rise free in Him."[12] Peter and Paul are recalled to the Romans as the leaders who hold the supreme authority over them, and this shows that, according to Ignatius, they had closer ties to Rome than to any other city. Ignatius knew, evidently, that they had come to Rome and had suffered martyrdom there. At least it is true that, writing to other cities in which no martyr had lived or suffered the supreme penalty, St. Ignatius does not mention any of the martyrs; and when he writes to the Christians of Ephesus, among whom only Paul had lived, he mentions only Paul.

But perhaps even clearer than the testimony of St. Clement and St. Ignatius is that which results from the close study of two Egyptian texts. These date apparently from the beginning of the second century, and were recently evaluated by a great student of ancient Christian literature, Erik Peterson.[13] They are two "prophetic" works of a literary type that began to enjoy wide favor at the end of the first century, a form best known through St. John's *Apocalypse*. They are entitled *The Ascension of Isaias* and *The Apocalypse of Peter*. In the first of these works it is predicted that Beliar (i.e., the devil) lord of the world, will descend from his firmament in the form of a matricidal man and destroy the seeds planted by the twelve apostles of the "Beloved" (i.e., of Christ), one of whom will fall into his hands.[14] The second work records certain words of Christ to Peter: "Behold, Peter, I have shown and exposed all things to you; and you must go into the capital of corruption and drink the chalice I have announced to you, from the hands of the son of him who is in Hades (i.e., of Satan who dwells in Hell), that his ruin may begin and that you may receive the fulfillment of the promises."[15]

The symbolic language could not be more transparent. The matricide mentioned in the first text is Nero, murderer of his own mother; the capital of corruption, alluded to in the second text, is Rome (as we have seen, St. Peter himself refers to it as "Babylon" in an Epistle), and that is where Peter must "drink the chalice," i.e., suffer martyrdom, thus beginning the downfall of the Antichrist, personified by Nero. It is clear that Peter's martyrdom in Rome, through the work of Nero, was already universally known in Egypt at the beginning of the second century.

If we continue to advance into the second century, testimonies of the martyrdom of Peter in Rome increase in number and in clarity. During the pontificate of Soter (165-174), Dionysus, Bishop of Corinth, wrote to the Romans recalling to them the teaching and martyrdom of Peter and Paul in Italy (i.e., in Rome). He added that their deaths occurred "on the same occasion" (κατὰ τὸν αὐτὸν καιρόν—*kata ton auton kairon*).[16] A few years later, the same information is offered by St. Irenaeus, Bishop of Lyons,[17] and several times by the Carthaginian apologist Tertullian.[18] To these concordant statements may be added that of the *Acts of Peter*, an account of the Apostle's activities composed in the Orient (perhaps in Syria) shortly after the middle of the second century. In this narration, there is a detailed account of the apostolate and martyrdom of Peter in the City. The Apostle is said to have been crucified and his body buried devoutly in the tomb of a follower of his, a certain senator Marcellus.[19]

It has been observed, and correctly so, that all of these notices which can be dated from the second half of the second century bring us back, implicitly, at least to the first half of the same century, since the tradition from which they derive could not have been formed on the spur of the moment, but must have taken some time to mature. Therefore, if they derive from the first half of the second century, it is possible to group them with the more ancient testimonies of St. Clement, St. Ignatius, *The Ascension of Isaias* and *The Apocalypse of Peter*. An uninterrupted chain is formed from the end of the first century to the second half of the second, and it continues, naturally growing stronger, into the succeeding century.

Some scholars believe that an allusion to the martyrdom of Peter and Paul in Rome can be found in the Apocalypse of St. John;[20] but the reasons given to sustain this thesis are not, according to others, sufficiently solid. The texts which tell us of the martyrdom of Peter in Rome are clearly numerous and eloquent enough to eliminate any doubt on the question. As for the form of martyrdom, there are strong reasons for asserting that Peter was crucified like his Master. This is the conclusion, as I have already observed, from a passage in the

Gospel of St. John.[21] The words in the *Acts of Peter,* composed, as we have seen, shortly after the middle of the second century, are even more explicit. And testimonies on the crucifixion of the Apostle multiply as time passes, not only from the Christians but also from their enemies. Thus, in the second half of the third century the Palestinian philosopher, Porphyry, an adversary of the Christians, believed firmly that Peter had been crucified.[22] The historian Tacitus, describing the horrible spectacle of Nero's persecution in a famous passage of the *Annals,* also tells us of Christians crucified (*crucibus affixi*)[23] and nothing prevents us from believing that among these crosses there could have been one on which Peter died. A tradition states that Peter wished, in his humility, to be crucified upside down. The information is very ancient, since the Alexandrian writer Origen already knew it at the beginning of the third century;[24] and, in succeeding centuries it became a favorite motif of pious Christian art (Fig. 5).

If we admit, as everything leads us to believe, that Peter was crucified during Nero's persecution, we must also necessarily recognize that the gardens of Nero were the site of the martyrdom. Tacitus, in the same passage of the *Annals,* mentions that the Christians were tortured in the gardens of Nero (and specially in the arena which was in those gardens), during the horrible spectacles which the emperor had arranged. Indeed, there was not, at that time, any other arena available or, at least, none appropriate for the purpose, since the Circus Maximus had been seriously damaged by the famous fire, which had in fact originated there, and the Circus Flaminius, even if it had not also been damaged by the fire, was too small and too tightly enclosed in the heart of the city to be used for Nero's grandiose plans.[25] The arena of Nero's garden, at the foot of the Vatican Hill, was, therefore, the most suitable, particularly since, after the fire, these

FIG. 3. St. Peter in the act of preaching. A mosaic which was formerly in the chapel of John VII (705-707), Vatican Grottoes.

very extensive gardens had been among the areas of Rome chosen by the Emperor to take care of the citizens who had lost their homes. Part of the exasperated lower classes, whom Nero wished to pacify with the torture of the Christians, could go to find amusement (if we may call it that) almost at their doorsteps.

But the logical deduction that Peter was crucified in that part of Rome is confirmed by other sources of information. An account of Peter's martyrdom, inspired by the *Acts of Peter* and falsely attributed to Linus, disciple and successor of the Apostle, informs us that Peter was crucified "near Nero's obelisk, by the hill."[26] This account is rather late, and certainly not written before the fourth century; but, as opposed to the *Acts of Peter,* composed in the Orient, it was written in Rome. Its information on the topography and local traditions of the City, therefore, deserves some attention. The author of this piece seems to believe that Peter was crucified in Nero's arena. Toward the end of the fourth century, St. Jerome states that Peter was crucified upside down "in the Vatican, near the Via Triumphalis."[27] The indication is obviously practically the same as that of Pseudo-Linus. This information is also confirmed by other sources. It is sufficient to mention the *Liber Pontificalis,* the classic history of the ancient Popes, which can be dated, in its most ancient form, in the sixth century. In Peter's biography it is stated that the Apostle was buried near the place where he had been crucified, i.e. "near the palace of Nero, in the Vatican, close to the Triumphalis region."[28] Since the "palace of Nero" is a fanciful term with which the Middle Ages identified the arena of Nero, and since the "Triumphalis region" is the zone adjacent to the Via Triumphalis, it can be seen that this report confirms the others.

Now let us consider the Apostle's tomb.

There is a tradition which holds that the tombs of Peter and Paul have been known and venerated since the time of St. John the Evangelist, i.e., since the time immediately following the martyrdom of the two Apostles. A sentence by the paganizing emperor Julian the Apostate (361-363) in his book *Against the Galileans,*[29] mentions this tradition. Julian observes that St. John first dared to give Jesus the title of God, and believes that he did it because he saw many of the Greek and Italian cities infested with the "disease" of Christianity and heard that the "memorials" (μνήματα—*mnemata*) of Peter and Paul, that is, their tombs, were venerated, if only in secret, by the faithful. We must note, however, that Julian introduces this bit of information with an "I believe" (οἶμαι —*oimai*). All that can be derived from it, therefore, is this:

that according to Julian, who was certainly better informed than we are on the ancient writers, the tombs of the Apostles were already venerated in the time of St. John.

According to some scholars, a direct testimony on the existence of Peter's tomb at Rome in the first half of the third century can be found in a passage of the apologist Tertullian in his book *On Modesty*.[30] In this work, Tertullian criticizes an unnamed bishop for absolving even those who have sinned against modesty, an absolution which, in his opinion, abuses the power to forgive sins given by Christ to Peter. "Perhaps," he says, addressing the bishop, "you think that the power of binding and loosing actually is derived from you, that is, from all the church close to Peter?" Identifying the unknown bishop with the Bishop of Rome, Callistus I, it has been conjectured that the expression "church close to Peter" refers to the privileged position of the Roman Church, formed and continuing to exist near the Apostle's tomb. This interpretation is not certain, but undoubtedly the words *"ecclesiam Petri propinquam"* might suggest a reference to memories of St. Peter's tomb.

Where was this tomb, according to the ancients? The *Acts of Peter,* written in the Orient shortly after 150 A.D., speak of the interment of Peter in the tomb of a senator, Marcellus, but they do not say where the tomb was located. The oldest and most important text that refers to Peter's tomb and indicates its location is the famous passage from Gaius. He was a churchman in Rome who lived at the time of Pope Zephyrinus (198-217) and became famous through a controversy with Proclus, a follower of the heretical Montanist sect. This controversy, which probably took place even before the reign of Zephyrinus, i.e., during the pontificate of Pope Victor I (186-197?), is known to us through a passage in the *Ecclesiastical History* of Eusebius, Bishop of Caesarea in Palestine. This passage can be dated between 312 and 315 A.D.[31] In the

FIG. 4. St. Peter with the keys. Mosaic which was formerly on the tomb of the Emperor Otto II (died 938). The Apostle is shown next to the seated Christ, who embraces him with His left arm. The image of St. Paul is on the other side of the Redeemer. From the Vatican Grottoes.

work of Eusebius are inserted the words of Gaius. Proclus, living in Asia Minor, had attempted to degrade the authority of the Church in Rome, asserting that Asia Minor possessed the tombs of various outstanding Christians, such as those— in the city of Hierapolis—of the Apostle Philip and his four daughters who were endowed with the prophetic spirit. Gaius, inflamed with zeal, replied to his adversary: "But I can show you the trophies of the Apostles. Indeed, if you wish to come to the Vatican or to the road to Ostia, you will find the trophies of those who have founded this Church."

The word "trophies" (τρόπαια—*tropaia*), used by Gaius, has been much discussed by scholars. According to the etymology of the word, the Greek term τρόπαιον (*tropaion*) indicates a monument commemorating the retreat (τροπή—*trope*) of the enemy and therefore the glory of the victor. Even the "tro-phies" of which Gaius speaks have undoubtedly a connota-tion of "victory"; on this point there is general agreement. But some scholars consider them merely "monuments of honor," admitting, at most, that they might indicate the place where the Apostles suffered martyrdom; other scholars, more accurately, give "trophies" the meaning of "tombs." And in fact the tomb of a Christian martyr, who has won his battle in the name of Christ, deserves to be considered a monument of victory, a "trophy." Besides, what could Gaius offer in op-position to the tombs of Philip and his daughters except other, much more glorious tombs? This interpretation, adopted by Eusebius himself in passing on the quotation from Gaius, is fully confirmed, as we shall see, by an epigraph found during the excavations under St. Peter's Basilica.[32] The testimony of Gaius tells us, then, that in the second half of the second cen-tury the tombs of Peter and Paul were honored in Rome, re-spectively in the Vatican and on the road to Ostia.

The fourth-century Roman author who wrote the *Martyr-dom of Saint Peter* (falsely attributed to Linus) records the place of the crucifixion, as we have seen, but does not mention the location of the tomb, stating only that the Martyr's body was taken down from the cross and placed in a new sarcophagus with the aid of the same senator Marcellus mentioned by the *Acts of Peter* in the second century.

Another fourth-century text, based on the *Acts of Peter*, gives a clue to the location of the tomb. This is a narrative attributed (another false attribution) to our friend, Marcellus the senator. We are told that Marcellus, helped by foreigners who had come from the Orient, secretly took Peter's body from the cross and placed it "under the terebinth near the Naumachia, in a place called Vatican."[33] The *Naumachia* was, in ancient times, a place on the Vatican plain where demonstrations of naval battles were held;[34] but the mention of the terebinth (a small tree that grows in dry places practically everywhere in the Mediterranean basin) is rather questionable. Certainly it would not be strange that St. Peter was buried under a terebinth tree, more so since the Vatican Hill must have been rich in vegetation at the time. But the terebinth is mentioned too often in the books of the Old Testament not to inspire a suspicion that we have here a bit of literary imitation. On the other hand, as we shall see later, there was a funeral monument in this same Vatican area which was called the *Terebinth* in the Middle Ages. The name was derived from the stone of Tivoli (tiburtine or, in the common language, travertine) with which it was built.[35] Be that as it may, the mention of the *Naumachia* and of the Vatican brings us, substantially, back to the same section of Rome.

There is also the information in the *Liber Pontificalis,* which cannot be dated before the sixth century. According to this text, Peter was buried "on the Via Aurelia, near the temple of Apollo, close to where he was crucified, near the palace of Nero, in the Vatican, near the Triumphalis region."

I have already explained this text in reference to the crucifixion of Peter;[36] and I shall speak of the "temple of Apollo"
later.[37] Here it is sufficient to point out that the *Liber Pontificalis* also places Peter's tomb in the Vatican, near the
"palace" of Nero, that is, near the arena in which the Apostle
had suffered martyrdom.

A detailed examination of the literary sources leads, as we
have seen, to a result that does not conflict with the tradition.
That is, it confirms that Peter came to Rome and suffered
martyrdom there under Nero; and it indicates the existence
of his tomb in precisely the place where the piety of the faithful has sought it and venerated it for so many centuries.

II

⌒

THE VATICAN IN ANCIENT TIMES

THE NAME "VATICAN" is derived from the Latin adjective *vaticanus,* which is derived, in turn, from the noun *Vatica* or *Vaticum.* This word is probably of Etruscan origin, a fact which can easily be explained when we consider that the region of the modern Vatican, on the right bank of the Tiber, originally belonged to Etruria, or rather, apparently, to the southernmost of the Etruscan cities, the powerful Veii with which Rome had to struggle so much during its first period of expansion. A memory of the very ancient allegiance of the Vatican to Etruria was still preserved in the first century A.D. Pliny the Elder, the famous naturalist who died in 79 A.D., a victim of the eruption of Vesuvius, tells us of a venerable oak in the Vatican region. An Etruscan inscription in bronze letters declared this oak sacred.[1]

When Veii fell under the power of the Romans (396 B.C.), the Vatican territory (Plate I) became part of the city of Rome, although it always remained outside the walls: the so-called Servian walls of the fourth century B.C. and, much later, the walls built by the emperors Aurelianus and Probus —between 270 and 278 A.D.—to defend the city against the fearful invasions of the barbarians. When the Emperor Augustus divided the city into fourteen regions, the Vatican became part of the fourteenth, which included the territory across the Tiber (trans Tiberim).

The Vatican zone was partly a hill and partly a plain. The heights, furrowed by deep gouges and called montes vaticani, are the hills which extend from Monte Mario to the Janiculum. The plain, lying between the hills and the Tiber, corresponds to the modern Prati di Castello, Borghi, Via della Conciliazione and all the right bank of the Tiber as far as the foot of the Janiculum Hill.

The terrain, covered by very permeable rocks through which rain water ran easily, was by nature poor and inhospitable; while the plain was subject to floods and, naturally, infested with malaria. Tacitus, speaking of the Emperor Vitellius' army which was decimated on the Vatican plain in the summer of 69, does not hesitate to call the Vatican region unhealthy (infamibus Vaticani locis).[2] Indeed, the Vatican plain was a worthy breeding-ground for snakes and became famous for them. According to Pliny there were snakes there of such enormous size that they were known to swallow babies whole.[3] The hilly region was even more poorly adapted for agriculture. Its wines, at least, had the reputation of being terrible, so much so that the poet Martial, in the second half of the first century A.D., compares them sometimes to vinegar, sometimes even to poison.[4] Its only resources consisted in some deposits of clay; these supplied many furnaces which turned out bricks, tiles, and some of the "fragile bowls" mentioned by the poet Juvenal (who lived between the first and second centuries A.D.) in one of his Satires.[5]

Nevertheless, this unhappy region of ancient Rome, during the first century A.D., caught the attention of various wealthy persons who tried to improve its conditions. Agrippina, wife of Germanicus and mother of the Emperor Caligula, had gardens planted there; the powerful family of the Domitii had other vast gardens nearby, and in particular Domitia Lepida, Nero's aunt who died in 59 A.D. as a result of poison given to her by her nephew. All these garden zones of green, which came through inheritance into the already immense patrimony of the debauched emperor, formed the vast "Gardens of Nero" (*horti Neronis*), the same in which, after the burning of Rome, Nero set up emergency housing for a large proportion of the homeless lower classes. Besides the "Gardens of Nero," there were also, perhaps, the very extensive gardens of M. Aquilius Regulus. We know, from an epistle of Pliny the Younger,[6] that this ambitious, plotting, cruel man, who lived from the time of Nero to the first years of Trajan, owned vast territories on the other side of the Tiber, arranged as gardens and adorned with large porticos and, on the river's bank, many statues. These gardens may have been located in the Vatican region.

It would be an error to think that this vast area was completely covered by true and proper gardens with rows of flowers, fountains, statues, and cages full of vari-colored birds. The region near the Tiber may have looked something like that, but the rest of the plain and the *montes vaticani* must have included large stretches of fields, forests and even sterile, uncultivated patches.

A territory this large would naturally have its streets and, in some places, buildings. The Vatican streets were named the Via Cornelia, the Via Aurelia and the Via Triumphalis, which all began at the Tiber and led to the heights. The so-called "Bridge of Nero," whose remains can still be seen near the modern Ponte Vittorio Emanuele, gave access to these streets. The name "Bridge of Nero" does not date back to Nero's time, but this is no reason to deny its accuracy. It is very probable that Nero, who owned extensive gardens in the Vatican area, would have a bridge built to connect this property with the rest of Rome. And it is equally probable that even before Nero's time, a bridge (perhaps a wooden rather than a stone one) crossed the Tiber at this point. In 134 A.D., Nero's bridge was joined by the Elian Bridge, whose purpose was to give access from the other side of the Tiber to the grandiose mausoleum of the Emperor Hadrian, now known as the Castel Sant' Angelo.

The most noteworthy structure on the Vatican plain was an arena built by the Emperor Gaius (i.e., Caligula: 37-41 A.D.) and improved by Nero (54-68 A.D.) and therefore known to the Romans as the *circus Gai et Neronis*. Caligula's successor, the Emperor Claudius, staged races and hunting shows in this arena several times, and Nero also used it quite frequently. Wishing to show the people his ability as a charioteer, as Tacitus informs us,[7] he enjoyed steering his horses in the "space marked off on the Vatican plain," that is, evidently, in the Vatican arena. In this same arena he staged the famous and very cruel spectacles which took the lives of so many Christian martyrs, among them, as we have reason to believe, St. Peter himself.[8] The chief landmark of the arena was the obelisk which Caligula had brought directly from Egypt on a ship, so beautiful that, according to Pliny, its equal had never before been seen.[9] This obelisk, we learn through an inscription dedicating it to the deceased emperors Augustus and Tiberius,[10] is the same that stands today in the center of St. Peter's Square. However, this is not its original location. We know that it was formerly located near the southern wall of the basilica, close to the modern Sacristy, and that in 1586, during the reign of Pope Sixtus V, it was moved by the architect Domenico Fontana into the center of the great square. This was a memorable project and its extreme difficulty led to some moments of drama. The record of this undertaking is preserved for us by a stone placed in the pavement at the spot from which the obelisk was taken.

But where, exactly, was the arena of Gaius and Nero in antiquity? Some scholars, thinking that the stone truly marks the original location of the obelisk and that it must have been located in the center of the arena, that is, at the middle of the so-called *spina* (dividing wall), believe that the oval area of the arena itself must have lain parallel to the Basilica of St. Peter. Others, although they admit that the obelisk was originally located on the spot indicated by the stone, do not find it necessary to believe that this spot was the center of the arena. Finally, there are others who believe that the obelisk was moved once before in ancient times, and that therefore the stone near the Sacristy merely indicates its second location, not its original site.

Recent excavations near the Sacristy have shown that this was, most probably, the original location of the obelisk. And it is difficult to believe that the obelisk would not have been placed on the *spina* in the arena, since the information we have on the structure of ancient arenas (for example, the largest arena in Rome, the Circus Maximus) show an almost universal custom of placing an obelisk right on the *spina*. It is very probable, therefore, that Nero's arena had its axis parallel to that of the future Basilica of St. Peter, with an opening toward the heights presently occupied by the Vatican Gardens. The nature of the terrain, which forms a small valley at this spot, would have naturally suggested the erection of an arena.

Except for the obelisk, no remains of the arena have come to light so far, but in this area the excavations have not gone so deep that we can say there are no traces. Besides, it is tenable that stone walls formed only part of the arena; the rest might have been formed of wooden panels or even of walls of vegetation, as was sometimes done during that period. At any rate, the existence of the arena in that area of the Vatican is proven by an epigraph found during the re-

FIG. 5. Tablet on the tomb of *C. Popilius Heracla* (first half of the second century A.D.). Excavations of the Vatican necropolis. (The words *in Vatic(ano) ad circum* can be read on lines 6 and 7.)

cent excavations under the basilica. The evidence is a marble tablet placed on the door of a sepulchre; the inscription on the tablet states that a certain C. Popilius Heracla had required his heirs to bury him in a mausoleum "in the Vatican near the arena" (*in Vaticano ad circum*) (Fig. 5). Since the mausoleum in which the heirs placed the remains of their benefactor is certainly that which the excavations discovered, we can deduce with certitude that the arena was in the immediate vicinity. And if we accept the very probable theory that the obelisk was formerly right on the *spina* of the arena, it is necessary to maintain that at the termination of the second century A.D. the arena was no longer used, since, to the West of the obelisk and right next to it, on a higher level, a circular-shaped tomb was built whose walls can be dated in the time of the Emperor Caracalla (211-217 A.D.). This tomb was later transformed into a church dedicated to St. Andrew (Fig. 7). The construction of this building on the site of the arena informs us that the arena no longer existed.

Besides the arena of Gaius and Nero, there was another place on the Vatican plain used for races: the *Gaianum,* named for the same Emperor Gaius (i.e., Caligula), and recorded by Dio Cassius, the Greek historian of Rome, who lived between the second and third centuries after Christ, as a "place" (χωρίον—*chorion*) where contests of horses were held.[11] Its location is still uncertain. Some scholars locate the *Gaianum* near Hadrian's tomb, others prefer to place it near the modern Via della Conciliazione, noting that in that area, and more exactly in the neighborhood of the church of Santa Maria in Traspontina, many charioteers' inscriptions have been found. At any rate, the report according to which the dissolute and extravagant Emperor Heliogabalus (218-222) once drove four teams of elephants on the Vatican plain, ruining the tombs in the area with his bad joke, probably refers not to the arena of Gaius and Nero but to the *Gaianum.*[12] It is hard to believe that anyone could drive four teams of elephants in the relatively restricted space of Nero's arena, not to mention the fact that in the time of Heliogabalus the arena must have been long out of use.

For those who enjoyed sea spectacles, the Vatican plain also offered the *Naumachia,* that is, a place set aside for the representation of naval battles.[13] The location of the Naumachia cannot be pointed out exactly; it is possible only to connect it with the medieval name of the chapel of San Pellegrino in Naumachia, located in the region of the modern Vatican City.

With the gardens and the places of spectacle there was also a sanctuary: the *Phrygianum,* i.e., a place where the

Phrygian divinities Cybele and Attis were honored. The first center of this cult in Rome was established on the Palatine, the most ancient of the seven hills, to commemorate the tradition according to which Aeneas, the progenitor of the Romans, came to the strands of Latium after his exile from Phrygian Troy. But another cult of Cybele and Attis settled later, outside the city's walls, right on the Vatican plain. The most ancient record we have of the Vatican Phrygianum is in an epigraph from 160 A.D.,[14] but it is very probable that the foundation of the sanctuary goes back to a more remote time. Its location cannot be established with perfect accuracy; but it is very probable that it was in the immediate vicinity of Nero's arena, near the modern Arco delle Campane. This seems proven by many foundations found in this area bearing reliefs and inscriptions referring to the characteristic cult of the Phrygian divinities (Fig. 7). In the various reliefs we find, besides the typical hat of Attis, bulls, sheep, pine trees,

Fig. 6. The obelisk from the arena of Gaius and Nero, in front of the round Church of St. Andrew. Drawing by the Netherlands artist Martin Van Heemskerk (1498-1574).

torches, flutes, reed pipes, drums and tambourines; all images
which speak for themselves. The inscriptions also tell us of
taurobolia, i.e., sacrifices of bulls which were—we might mention—the culminating act of these horrid and mysterious
rites.[15] The cult of Attis and Cybele in the Vatican lasted a
long time, almost throughout the fourth century A.D., when
the basilica built by Constantine to honor Peter already stood
nearby. But we have reason to believe that the celebration of
these bloody rites was suspended for a fairly long period during the fourth century, not only because these rites were far
removed from the spirituality of Christianity, now publicly
professed throughout the Empire, but also because the *Phrygianum* was in the middle of the storage-yard for the construction of the basilica. The dates found on the inscriptions
recording the *taurobolia* are therefore very valuable in help-
ing to establish the chronology of Constantine's basilica, and
permit us to fix the beginning of construction around 322
A.D.[16]

Fig. 7. Base from the sanctuary of the Phrygian de-
ities (fourth century A.D.).
Vatican Grottoes. On the
two panels of the relief can
be seen a bull, flutes, a pine
tree from which a drum
and a syrinx hang, two
crossed torches and other
objects related to the cult.

The *Liber Pontificalis,* whose first version goes back to the sixth century, asserts that Peter was buried "near the temple of Apollo" and specifies that this "temple of Apollo" was in the Vatican, near "Nero's palace."[17] Since we must certainly identify "Nero's palace" with the ruins of the famous arena, the temple of Apollo must have been very near the present basilica or precisely in the area which it covers. But scholars' attempts to track down the remains of the temple of Apollo have been so far unsuccessful and will probably remain so, since it is quite possible that the statement in the *Liber Pontificalis* may be unfounded and the temple of Apollo may never have existed.

There were also tombs in the ancient Vatican region. At first, the presence of tombs close to gardens and places of amusement such as the arena, the *Gaianum,* and the *Naumachia,* may seem strange; but on further reflection it is easy to recognize that our reluctance to mingle life and death by burying the dead next to places where living is most intense

Fig. 8. Monument of *Nunnius, Ma* and *Crescens* (first century A.D.). Excavations in the Vatican parking lot.

derives from a modern concept far from the mentality of the ancients. The Romans of the imperial age did not have this kind of attitude and saw nothing wrong in laying their dead to rest where the survivors dwelt or sought amusement. For example, it is sufficient to recall that on the Appian Way the rich villa of the Quintilii stands out flanked by tombs and that in "Caesar's gardens" on the right bank of the Tiber there are tombs right next to other buildings that have nothing funereal about them.

Students of Roman topography know that for the ancient Romans the sides of highways were favorite burial places. Thus, long lines of tombs, decorated with varying degrees of ostentation, bordered not only the Appian Way but also the Via Latina, the Via Prenestina and all the great arteries which radiated from the City to the near and far places of the world dominated by Rome. Sometimes the tombs were so close together that they formed cemeteries. The same thing happened, and it was natural that it should happen, along the streets of the Vatican region.

Many years ago, sporadic excavations had already shown the existence of an ancient burial place along the Via Triumphalis and its various side streets, i.e., in the area between the Vatican Palaces and the modern Piazza Risorgimento. A recent excavation, executed systematically in the Vatican City, in the place where the parking lot now stands, has confirmed the existence of this necropolis, bringing to light some tombs of very great interest and showing that the greatest growth of the necropolis took place in the first century A.D. Among other documents, one that stands out is the beautiful monument which a certain Nunnius, a slave of Nero, had made for himself, his wife who had the rare name *Ma,* and his son *Crescens* (Fig. 8).

This large and important burial place extended across the northeastern slope of the hill on which the Vatican Palaces

are built. But even on the southern slope, along the Via
Cornelia and its side streets, there were tombs. A notable
part of them, which I shall discuss later at greater length,
came to light during excavations under St. Peter's Basilica.
Other tombs were located, more to the west, behind the apse
of the basilica, in the place now occupied by the chapel of
St. Stephen of the Abyssinians; still others, more to the east,
in front of the basilica. In all probability, two funeral monuments which were well-known in the Middle Ages and have
since been destroyed, the so-called *Meta Romuli* and the
Terebintus belonged to this row of tombs (Fig. 9). The
first structure, considered by popular imagination to be
the tomb of Romulus, founder of Rome, was a building in the
form of a pyramid, covered by large marble slabs which were
used in the seventh century to beautify the atrium of St.
Peter's; the second, called *Terebintus* (a deformation of
Tiburtinus) from the stone of Tivoli (travertino) which had
been used in its construction, was circular in form.

The rich tombs discovered under St. Peter's Basilica are
not older than 130 A.D., approximately, and this discovery
by the excavators has some importance in studying the question of St. Peter's tomb. Indeed, some scholars, noting the
absence of first-century tombs in this area, have found the
fact sufficient reason to deny point-blank the presence of the
Apostle's tomb. But further investigations have shown that
some tombs were there even in the first century.[18] The *Meta
Romuli*, with its pyramidal form similar to that of the well-
known pyramid of Gaius Cestius on the Via Ostiense (which,
by the way, was taken for the tomb of Remus in the Middle
Ages), seems to have been a first-century structure, very suitable to the taste of the times in which the Roman emperors,
deeply interested in Egyptian things, were bringing venerable obelisks to Rome and encouraging the imitation of
Egyptian styles. A group of first-century tombs must have

FIG. 9. The *Meta Romuli* and the *Terebintus,* panel of the bronze door executed for St. Peter's Basilica by Antonio Averlino, called Philaretes (from 1433 to 1445). The scene shows the crucifixion of St. Peter before the eyes of Nero. At the bottom can be seen (left to right): the *Meta Romuli* (before which the goddess Roma sits), Hadrian's tomb (now the Castel Sant'Angelo), and the *Terebintus.*

existed on the site of the present chapel of St. Stephen of the Abyssinians. This fact is demonstrated by a funeral inscription (Fig. 10) set up by freed slaves of the Emperor Domitian between 83 and 96 A.D. and other documents which can be dated either in the time of the Flavii (69-96) or even in earlier times. Other first-century tombs have also been found in the area of the modern St. Peter's Square and near the southern side of the basilica. Thus, we can establish the existence of a line of first-century tombs which leaves the Tiber, follows the route of the modern Via della Conciliazione, crosses St. Peter's Square and, passing under the basilica, reaches the site of St. Stephen of the Abyssinians and the slopes of the Vatican hills.

In opposition to those scholars who have denied the existence of first-century tombs under the basilica, we can state with certitude today that there were first-century tombs there. From earlier excavations one tomb was already known, covered with tiles among which was one with the manufacturer's mark (Fig. 11) datable in the reign of the Emperor Vespasian (69-79).[19] It was possible to object (and naturally some did

FIG. 10. Tomb inscription set up by freedmen of the Emperor Domitian (83-96). On the south side of the Church of St. Stephen of the Abyssinians. The name of Domitian is found on lines 2ff: *Imp(eratoris) Caesaris (Domiti)ani Aug(usti) Germanici.*

FIG. 11. Seal from the time of Vespasian (69-79). Excavations of the Vatican necropolis. The seal reads: *Stat(ius) Marcius Demetrius f(ecit)*.

object) that this single tile might have been second-hand, and therefore taken from somewhere else. But now new proof has been added to the marked tile, and it is even more conclusive: a small lamp also marked and found in a place close to the tomb bearing the mark from the time of Vespasian. The lamp is made of terra cotta and belonged to a tomb, a fact deduced from the presence of burned bones and other fragmentary objects related to funeral rites: pieces of another lamp, vases, glasses, etc. The presence of burned bones and of many pieces of ash indicates that the tomb to which the inscribed lamp belonged was used for cremation and that the funeral material in its vicinity was the contents of a crematory furnace (*ustrinum*). Now, our lamp is marked with the name of the potter *L. Munatius Threptus*. The same mark occurs on many other lamps, two of which can be dated with certitude in the first century, thanks to a lucky discovery. Some of these lamps were found in the tomb of the Statilii near the Porta Maggiore, which was closed in the time of Statilia Messalina, third wife of Nero, about 70 A.D. It follows that the lamp found under the basilica of St. Peter belongs to the first century, and this conclusion is confirmed by the examination of other funeral materials found in the vicinity which can also be dated in the first century.

In conclusion, it is evident that burials did take place, during the time of St. Peter, in the area where later a basilica was to be built in his honor. Thus, the location of the Apostle's tomb in the place where tradition would have it, is not, in itself, a strange or anachronistic idea. There were probably no large, rich mausoleums in this part of the Vatican plain during the first century. These were built in great numbers during the following century, changing radically the aspect of the region. In the first century, there must have been only poor and meager tombs, with barely the width of a street (evidently the Via Cornelia) separating them from the neighboring arena of Gaius and Nero. They were the tombs of poor people, and among them the tomb of the Fisherman from Galilee could easily have found its place.

Fig. 12. View of the Tomb of the Valerii during the excavation work. Excavations of the Vatican cemetery.

III

~

THE NECROPOLIS UNDER
THE BASILICA

THE BASILICA built by the Emperor Constantine in honor of the Apostle remained substantially intact for many centuries. About the middle of the fifteenth century, Pope Nicholas V decided to replace the original apse with another much more ornate one. But it was not until 1506 that the humanist Pope Julius II commissioned Bramante to undertake a sweeping change, that is, to tear down the old building and to supplant it with a new one inspired by the renewed classical ideals of the Renaissance. The work took more than a century. Finally, on November 18, 1626, Pope Urban VIII was able to consecrate the new church. Already, work had begun on the magnificent bronze baldacchino of Gianlorenzo Bernini, inaugurated by the same Urban VIII on June 28, 1633.

The work on the new building had presented several opportunities to cast a fleeting look under the foundations of the basilica. In 1574, during the pontificate of Gregory XIII, while working on the foundations of some columns in front of the papal altar, workmen discovered a tomb decorated with mosaics. The canonist Tiberio Alfarano, reporting on this excavation, notes that the tomb was "all in ancient mosaics with figures that seemed to be horses," and he adds that the surroundings, almost filled with mortar or earth, contained a "marble platform on which there was a dead body surrounded and covered by pure lime to preserve it." Alfarano thought that this body was probably the corpse of a Christian fallen from the level of the basilica through an opening still visible in the ceiling. As I shall demonstrate in a moment, it is quite probable that the mosaic described by Alfarano is the same one that was discovered during the recent excavation in the Christian tomb of the Julii.

More discoveries were made in 1615, during the work for the foundations of the modern Confessione. We have information on this excavation from the description published in 1618 by the canonist Francesco Maria Torrigio and from a sketch engraved in 1635 by the architect Benedetto Drei. The *Liber Pontificalis,* edited in the sixth century, had fixed in many minds the idea that St. Peter's close successors, Linus, Cletus, etc., were buried next to Peter's tomb. The seventeenth century excavators were therefore prepared to find these venerable tombs. Thus we find Torrigio speaking of the finding of the tomb of a Pope dressed in a chasuble and pallium, and in Drei's sketch we find pictures of various corpses with this description: "These Pontiffs, marked with fasces and crosses, are Saints Linus, Cletus, Anacletus, Euaristus" etc. It was also believed that Pope Linus' epitaph had been found, but it has not come down to us.

Besides the tombs of the presumed Popes, other tombs were found, among them one from which a sweet aroma came forth. Coins from the time of Constantine, marked with the Cross, and various other objects were also found. These excavations of 1615 did not get down to the virgin soil, and perhaps not even down to the pagan stratum, but they did bring to light a small part of the burial place which had been formed under the basilica built by Constantine.

The excavations of 1626, made for the foundations of the Bernini baldacchino, went deeper. Begun on June 29, 1626, from the southeast corner of the papal altar, these were described by the canonist Ugo Ubaldini and by the author of an anonymous diary now preserved in the archives of St. Peter's. The excavations brought many tombs to light, reaching the pagan necropolis at various points. In one of these tombs, explored more deeply by recent excavations, there was found a sarcophagus that aroused great interest at the time. On the lid was represented a man lying on a couch with a cup in his hand, and on the front of the sarcophagus was carved an epigram in which the deceased, a certain *Flavius Agricola,* a native of Tibur (Tivoli), stated his theories as a devout epicurean. These beliefs differed considerably from those of his wife, who died before him, a good and pious woman who had been initiated into the mysteries of the Egyptian Isis.[1] The pleasure-loving Tiburtine's verses caused such a scandal in 1626 that it was found necessary to throw the sarcophagus into the Tiber, but not without first copying the famous epigram which has thus been preserved for us.

It appears that the 1626 investigations reached virgin soil. But the researches ended abruptly as soon as the purpose of giving solid foundations for the columns of the bronze baldacchino had been accomplished. An irresistible prudence, almost an unconfessed fear, prevented a thorough investigation of the terrain. The fear of finding something down there which would contradict or modify the tradition dear to the faithful overcame the desire to appease a burning curiosity. It seemed better, all things considered, to respect the veil of prudent silence which the centuries had woven over St.

Peter's tomb and to leave intact in faithful minds a consoling though unproven certitude.

Not until our own century did the time seem ripe to begin the memorable undertaking, and Pope Pius XII had the distinction of beginning it in the name of Science and of Faith.

The idea of systematically exploring the ground under the Vatican basilica may have appealed to Pius XII many years before he was raised to the Papal throne. But the real impulse came to him just before he was elected to the papacy, from the works undertaken between February 10 and 20, 1939 to prepare the tomb of Pius XI. In his will, Pius XI had expressed a wish to be buried in the Vatican Crypt, near the tomb of Pius X and as close as possible to the Confessione area. To satisfy the dead Pontiff's wishes, an excavation was made along the southern wall of the Crypt. This excavation brought to light some traces of the burial place which lay underneath. This was, so to speak, the first breach in the wall of centuries. Cardinal Eugenio Pacelli, having become Pope Pius XII, decided to continue what had been begun, and on June 28, 1939, vigil of the feast of the Apostles Peter and Paul, he gave the order for the investigations. So far, there have been two phases to this work. The first was carried out without interruption during the decade from 1939 to 1949, and concluded with the Holy Year, 1950. The second opened in 1953 and still continues.

The ancient street (probably the *Cornelia*) which ran from the Tiber to the heights of the *montes vaticani*[2] followed a route corresponding to the modern Via della Conciliazione, St. Peter's Square, the apse of the basilica, and the site of the present church of St. Stephen of the Abyssinians. As I have explained in dealing with the Vatican in antiquity,[3] there were already tombs along this road in the first century

A.D. At the site of the modern basilica, the road must have been flanked on the left by the arena of Gaius and Nero; but on the right, even in this area of amusement, the line of tombs continued. At this point, the tombs must have been relatively poor and unpretentious, and perhaps this is the reason why, in the first half of the second century, large and rich mausoleums began to crowd into the same place.

This group of tombs constitutes the large burial place uncovered by the 1939-1949 excavations at about seven meters below the level of the basilica. (Plate II). Constantine's bold plan of building a temple in this place to honor the Apostle made it necessary—about 322 A.D.—to fill in the old burial place with soil and rubble, placing powerful foundations here and there, and creating a new level from which the basilica would rise. The part of the burial place uncovered by the excavations, with long and painstaking work, corresponds to a line in the present church running from the Confessione to the Blessed Sacrament Chapel. The excavation has stopped here, but the necropolis certainly continues (as I have already explained) to the east toward the square and to the west toward the apse of the basilica and the site of the small church of St. Stephen of the Abyssinians.

The pre-Constantinian necropolis is, in general, pagan; but there are traces of Christianity other than the archaeological and epigraphical documents concerning St. Peter. This simultaneous presence of pagan and Christian elements is a characteristic that distinguishes the Vatican necropolis from other contemporary cemeteries, particularly from the one of the Sacred Isle near Ostia which resembles it so much in other ways.

Let us first glance at the pagan part of the Vatican necropolis, before concentrating on the Christian elements.

The first thing that strikes a visitor in the necropolis is the double file of tombs separated by a narrow road (Fig.

FIG. 13. Road between the tombs in the Vatican necropolis.

13). The age of these small buildings seems to vary from about 130 to about 300 A.D. Well made of brick, with occasional openings in the wall formed of small rhomboid-shaped stones (*opus reticulatum*), the tombs have decorous façades with thresholds of travertine and marble tablets set in above

FIG. 14. Marble tablet above the entrance to the tomb of the Valerii (second half of the second century A.D.). Excavations of the Vatican necropolis. The name of *C. Valerius Herma,* owner of the tomb, can be read clearly.

the entrances to indicate, in neat inscriptions, the names of the owners (Fig. 14). Sometimes the architects saw fit to beautify the exteriors of the tombs with terra cotta decorations or with fine mosaic pictures (Fig. 15). In some cases, the interiors have stairs ingeniously cut into the walls to give access to upper stories or to a street lying on a higher level. The interiors have, naturally, plaster decorations, pictures or mosaics (Fig. 16), and sometimes contain sarcophagi of terra cotta or marble.

The numerous inscriptions tell us that the inhabitants of this city of the dead were, for the most part, people who could not claim noble origins. The Greek surnames joined to

Roman family names (*Valerii, Iunii, Caetennii, Popilii* and so forth) show that these are freedmen who, in more or less recent times, had been given their freedom (and, with freedom, the family name) by their respective owners and benefactors. But if their social status was quite modest, they had, in compensation, ample economic opportunities, undoubtedly derived from the practice of crafts and commerce. This economic position allowed them to build tombs of exquisite elegance for themselves and their deceased relatives. Very rarely do the inscriptions in this necropolis tell us of people who held public office, and truly exceptional is the mention of a *consul designatus,* a certain *Ostorius Euhodianus.* He is mentioned, as father of the deceased, in the inscription carved on the sarcophagus of *Ostoria Chelidon* (Fig. 17), a woman

FIG. 15. Mosaic picture showing the killing of Pentheus by the Maenads (end of the second century A.D.). Excavations of the Vatican necropolis. The scene shows the Maenads and a panther attacking the pine tree on which Pentheus, a king of Thebes hostile to Dionysus, has taken refuge.

who gracefully joined to her father's family name (*Ostoria*) the Greek name of the swallow (*chelidon*). When the sarcophagus was opened, after so many centuries, by the excavators of the necropolis, the dead woman's body was found richly embalmed, dressed in purple and wrapped in a shroud interwoven with gold.

All the inscriptions of the pagan necropolis offer us interesting data for better understanding of the society and the life of those times. Among others, a very important epigraph is found set into the wall above the entrance to a tomb which has not yet been completely excavated: that of *C. Popilius Heracla*. As I have already mentioned,[4] this epigraph reports the provision in the man's will which required his heirs to build him a tomb *in Vaticano ad circum;* and therefore preserves the record, so precious for us, of that Circus of Nero so closely connected with St. Peter's life.

But perhaps the most interesting thing in this ancient Roman pagan necropolis is the access which it gives us to the religious ideas and sentiments of those who used it. It is appropriate to speak briefly of these pagan concepts before rising, with Christian ideas, to a higher sphere.

Two types of burial rite were practiced in this cemetery: cremation, and the placing of the body in the earth or in a sarcophagus. Thus, the walls of the tombs usually contain small niches with urns for the ashes of the deceased, and in the same tombs, there are usually large repositories in which the bodies were piously placed, either in empty spaces formed with tiles or in true and proper sarcophagi of varying quality. In a niche in the tomb of the Valerii, the expression *tibi sit* can be read clearly carved in the plaster covering the wall. The one who wrote it may have been thinking of the very common wish that the Romans loved to apply to their deceased: *tibi sit terra levis* ("may the earth be light upon you"); but he stopped after the *sit,* thinking that this for-

FIG. 16. Interior of the tomb of the Cetennii (middle of the second century A.D.). Excavations of the Vatican necropolis.

mula, very appropriate for those buried in the earth, had no meaning for a person reduced to a few handsful of ashes in a vase. Some urns in the same tomb of the Valerii have preserved for us—a point of great interest—the death-mask taken on the face of the deceased before its features disappeared forever on the funeral pyre.

But whichever burial rite was used—cremation or inhumation—it seems that in general there was a firmly-rooted belief in the survival of souls and the joys they would experience in another world. But ideas on this subject were not very clear; various concepts were intertwined together, with frequent shifts of emphasis.

Above all, there was the idea that the deceased dwelt in the tomb, prolonging, in a way, the life he had led on earth. This is the reason for the care shown by survivors to make this new dwelling pleasant, painting on the walls and vaults, pictures of flowers (particularly roses), birds, and vases full of vividly colored fruit. Evidently they wished the dead to continue enjoying what they had most loved on earth. And thinking that after the toils of mortal life rest must be sweet, they liked to put pictures of graceful spirits on the walls, with poppies from whose seeds—it was believed—the blessing of easy sleep would rain down upon the dead (Fig. 18).

But if the bodies remained physically in the tombs, did the souls also stay there? Or did they go off to dwell somewhere else, in distant, mysterious lands? On the floor of one tomb there is a mosaic showing the symbolic scene of the maiden Proserpina, abducted by Pluto, god of the dark underworld, while she was gathering flowers (Fig. 19). This scene agrees very well with the belief, widespread among the ancients, that the souls of the dead went beneath the earth into the silent kingdom of Avernus, to wander there, pale shadows, in darkness. On the walls of other tombs are shown idyllic landscapes, or cornucopias overflowing with flowers, fruits and corn: pictures which seem to refer to those far-off isles of the blest to which—according to another idea—the souls set out, anxious to enjoy at last a serene life in a perpetual holiday of light and joy. Other walls of the necropolis show us painted pictures of Psyche and of little Cupids; and these pretty winged beings remind us that, according to an idea fairly common at the time, spirits flew into the sky, to find their final resting place among the stars or in the halo of the moon's silvery light.

Corresponding to this variety of ideas about life beyond the tomb there is a variety of religious currents which met and mingled at this time. This variety is well demonstrated in the plaster ornaments in the tomb of the Valerii. There, beside Minerva, the wise goddess of Olympus, can be seen Isis, Apollo Harpocrates and Jupiter Dolichenus, three exotic divinities very dear to the Romans of the imperial period;

Fig. 17. Sarcophagus of *Ostoria Chelidon* (third century A.D.). Excavations of the Vatican necropolis.

while satyrs and maenads proclaim, with their frenzied dances, the invincible power of that Dionysus-Bacchus whom the pagan society of the time considered a symbol of supreme happiness in earthly life and also in the future world. It might even be said that the religion of Dionysus predominates in this silent city of the dead. The young Dionysus, with his gay cortege of satyrs and maenads, his panthers and his thrysus and his festive, heavily-loaded bunches of grapes, seems to promise, from the walls of tombs and from the carvings on marble sarcophagi, the end of troubles in an eternal, happy drunkenness. (Fig. 20).

This was, approximately, the spiritual milieu in which the elements of the new Faith came to find their place. Side by side with the dead pagans in this necropolis, Christians found their eternal rest. This promiscuity sprang, undoubtedly, from the desire of the faithful to place their dead in a cemetery which, as they firmly believed, held the sacred remains of the Apostle Peter.

What are the Christian elements which, not including references to St. Peter, have been found so far in the Vatican necropolis?

A very important Christian document is preserved for us in the tomb of the Valerii; but, since it also concerns St. Peter, I propose to speak of it later.[5] There are also some compartments found in the tomb of the Matuccii which may be Christian, as, most probably, are the many resting places revealed by the latest excavations under the pavement in the tomb of the Valerii. There are also, here and there, funeral inscriptions which clearly refer to the new Faith. Thus, a mutilated epigraph found in the so-called tomb of the Egyptian (because of a fresco representing the sparrow-headed Egyptian god Horus) is shown to be Christian by the formula *in pace* followed by a palm symbol. Similarly, in the tomb of the Cetennii, there are unquestionably Christian inscriptions: the epigraph of a certain Siricius (a favorite Christian name in the early centuries) and the moving epitaph of *Aemilia*

FIG. 18. Spirits with poppies, a plaster ornament in an arch of the tomb of the Valerii (second half of the second century). Excavations of the Vatican necropolis.

Fig. 19. Mosaic depicting the abduction of Proserpina (third century A.D.). Excavations of the Vatican necropolis.

Gorgonia (Fig. 21) a woman, according to the inscription, of "remarkable beauty and chastity." The stone is decorated with the customary motif of doves and with the unusual figure of a woman taking water from a well. The artist certainly wished this scene to represent the soul of the pious dead woman receiving the symbolic water of eternal refreshment. Other Christian epitaphs have been found in the tomb of the Valerii. The epitaph carved on the sarcophagus of one *Valerinus Vasatulus* must be considered Christian particularly because of the fact that it mentions the date on which the deceased was placed in the tomb. Among the Christians, the day of burial was considered worthy of being recorded as a happy event, since it opened the gates of Paradise for the soul, while among the pagans the custom was to avoid mentioning it since it was considered a cause of everlasting sorrow. Another stone in the tomb of the Valerii, shown to be Christian by the presence of the sign of the Redeemer (⳨), records a man of good character who, as a true Christian, had

FIG. 20. Sarcophagus showing the triumph of Dionysus (second century A.D.). Excavations of the Vatican necropolis.

passed his life in perfect happiness: "he joked with everyone and never had quarrels."

But besides these stones which speak with suggestive frankness the language of the Faith, the necropolis has preserved for us an entirely Christian tomb which constitutes one of its greatest attractions. It is the tomb of the Julii, which was inserted between two older tombs, using their side walls. Belonging originally to pagans, as is indicated by the remains of some urns for ashes, it soon became a Christian tomb and was richly decorated with splendid mosaics. The transformation seems to have taken place in the first half of the third century. The brilliant mosaics which decorated the walls and the ceiling are now mostly fallen away, but the tesserae have left traces in the plaster, showing the design of the figures which have been lost. And the remaining section of the mosaic has a remarkable beauty and liveliness.

The Christians who owned this tomb wished to have symbolic scenes of deep and consoling significance represented in it. On the left wall, the Good Shepherd, with a sheep across his shoulders, recalls the infinite mercy of Christ to men. Next, facing the entrance, is the picture of the divine Fisherman, a symbol of Baptism which regenerates souls. On the right wall is seen the motif of the prophet Jonas, swallowed by the sea monster and released after three days from the prison of that dark gullet; an allusion to the mystery of the Redeemer who descended into Hell and rose to the glory of heaven after three days, a happy guarantee for souls that, living in Christ, hope to rise with Him. The joy of the hoped-for resurrection is also expressed, on the ceiling of the tomb, by the majestic figure of Christ the sun rising radiantly above a chariot with white horses to the place of eternal happiness. (Fig. 22). These are precisely the horses seen, as I have mentioned, in the sixteenth century by the canonist Tiberio Alfarano, during a chance exploration under the basilica's floor;[6] even the hole in the ceiling is there, just as Alfarano described it.

Today, the figure of Christ the sun is the best-preserved part of the mosaic. According to a motif which was also used earlier by the pagans to represent the apotheosis of an emperor, the chariot of Christ ascends in a glorious light, expressed by a background composed of gleaming yellow tesserae; from the corners of the tomb rise the emerald branches of a vine, a symbol which reminds the faithful that they are

FIG. 21. Christian epitaph of *Aemilia Gorgonia* (third century A.D.). Excavations of the Vatican necropolis. At left, the deceased is shown drawing the water of life. Above the picture is written: *anima dulcis Gorgonia*.

FIG. 22. Mosaic showing Christ-the-sun on the ceiling of the tomb of the Julii (first half of the third century A.D.). Excavations of the Vatican necropolis.

united in Christ, the mystical vine, and that also tells them of the joys of the Eucharist, the beginning of the unending "Eucharistia" which the faithful will enjoy in the next world. The vines of Dionysus have now become an eloquent symbol of Christian hope.

This richly ornamented expression of faith might seem strange in a small tomb wedged in and almost suffocated in the middle of the necropolis. But if we consider it more carefully it is not hard to find the reason that justifies—very fully —the money and the care expended by the owners of this tomb within its narrow walls. This motive was—without doubt—the immediate proximity of Peter's Memorial.

IV

THE APOSTLE'S MEMORIAL

PILGRIMS WHO CROSS the threshold of the Vatican basilica usually go right to the papal altar. This, precisely, is the goal of their journey, since there—they know—is the place sacred to St. Peter.

In the center of the area over which Michelangelo's magnificent dome rises, the altar stands majestically above the level of the basilica, protected by the very rich bronze baldacchino, the canopy supported by the ornate columns of Gianlorenzo Bernini. At the foot of the altar, toward the east, is the entrance of the Confessione, a sort of open chapel, gleaming with marble and enclosed by a railing on which, day and night, eighty-nine oil lamps gleam in holders of gilded bronze. The faithful, prostrated around the railing, see down in the Confessione where a beautiful marble statue of Pope Pius VI, sculptured by Antonio Canova, kneels in prayer.

The Pontiff prays facing toward the rear wall of the Confessione, where the papal altar rises (Fig. 23). But what is the object of his prayers? What is there in that wall? There is a rich bronze door, behind which is the so-called Nicchia dei

FIG. 23. The stairway to the Confession under the Papal Altar with the bronze columns which support the canopy (not shown in the photograph). The back of Pope Pius VI is shown as he kneels facing the rear wall of the Confession.

Pallii (Niche of the Pallia), a small empty place in which, following a centuries-old tradition, are deposited the sacred insignia (*pallia*) which the Pope bestows on some Bishops. And certainly there is some significance in the fact that the insignia of pastors of souls are put in this place which represents, for the faithful, the heart of the basilica and, at the same time, of all Christendom. In fact, the papal altar under which the Nicchia dei Pallii is found, rises on a series of superimposed constructions in the most sacred part of the Vatican.

Now let us go down, step by step, to see what is under the altar. And as we go down, it is easy to see that we are also going back through the centuries.

Under the present altar, which belongs to the time of Clement VIII (1592-1605), is the altar of Callistus II (1119-1124); lower still, that of Gregory the Great (590-604). Next we find the monument built in honor of St. Peter by the Emperor Constantine after his victory near the Milvian Bridge (October 28, 312) and the establishment of peace with the Church by the Edict of Milan (313 A.D.). The date of this monument cannot be fixed with absolute certainty, but there are good reasons to think that it preceded the construction of the basilica (begun about 322) and perhaps it is no later than 315; that is, the year in which great holidays were held in Rome to exalt Constantine and his victory; the year in which Rome dedicated the famous Arch of Triumph which still rises majestically from its soil.

Constantine's monument to Peter contained within its rich marble construction an earlier chapel* which has been brought to light by excavations. This chapel indicates, evidently, the place sacred to the Apostle, the place that Constantine considered so important and worthy of honor that he did not hesitate to build on it first his precious monument

---

* Or, more literally, shrine. M.G.

and later—at the cost of incalculable expense and enormous labor—the great basilica.

The characteristic chapel rises from the level of the ancient necropolis already described. It stands in a little open area, a sort of small square in the middle of various tombs.** This little area which, in relation to the modern basilica, is directly under the Confession, was called "Field P" by the excavators. It is rectangular in form (about seven meters from north to south, about four from east to west), and it lies in a place where the terrain rises quite rapidly from the south to the north, i.e. toward the Apostolic Palaces, and more gradually from the east to the west, i.e., toward the Vatican Gardens.

Field P is bounded on the west by a wall called "Red" because of the red color of the plaster (now largely fallen off) which was used to cover it; on the south by a tomb which the excavators call S; on the east, but only in the southern half of the east section, by another tomb called O (this tomb was owned by the Matuccii and is sometimes called by their name). The northern boundary of the eastern side and all the northern boundary cannot be traced today, but there are good reasons for believing that there were once structures there which have been mostly destroyed.

Behind the Red Wall ran a small street (the so-called *clivus*) which slopes up from south to north and includes some sets of stairs (Fig. 24). On the other side of this *clivus* are the remains of two other tombs, called R and R¹ by the excavators. The *clivus* gave access to the Tomb R¹ and to a tomb called Q which lies behind the Red Wall with the Red Wall itself used for its eastern wall.

Under the *clivus* runs a little gutter used for drainage and covered with a line of tiles, five of which, fortunately, bear a mark by which they can be dated. The mark mentions

** See Plate III.

FIG. 24. A view of the *clivus* behind the Red Wall. Excavations of the Vatican necropolis. At left are the remains of Tombs R and R[1]: at the rear, the stairs; at right, the brick facing of Tomb S and part of the back surface of the Red Wall. The sarcophagus decorated with curved lines and reliefs sank down from the level of Constantine's basilica.

Aurelius Caesar (the future Emperor Marcus Aurelius) and his wife Faustina as proprietors of the furnace in which the tiles were made.[1] The tiles can therefore be dated between about 146 and 161 A.D. It was about 146 when Faustina, wife of the future Emperor Marcus Aurelius, received the title of Augusta, and in 161 Aurelius Caesar, having succeeded Antoninus Pius, abandoned the name of Aurelius Caesar and took that of Marcus Aurelius.

The essential purpose of the Red Wall seems to have been to fix the boundaries of the various burial places in the area. From this fact, it can be considered contemporary with the gutter I have mentioned, and therefore it can be dated between about 146 and 161 A.D. In round numbers, and wishing to take the latest possible date, we can say that it was built by about 160 A.D.

The most ancient of the tombs surrounding Field P is certainly Tomb O, which, as can be seen from the marble tablet over the entrance, belonged to the Matuccii family. This tomb, in which the rite of cremation was practiced, can be dated about 130, and is certainly later than 123, since a brick was found in one of its walls with a seal dating from that year.

The Tomb S, which bounds all the southern flank of Field P, contains traces of cremation urns and of repositories for inhumation. Later than Tomb O, Tomb S is still earlier than the Red Wall, since the wall leans on it, thus barring access to Field P from the south. Therefore Tomb S can be assigned a date somewhere between 130 and 150.

Tomb R, built on the other side of the *clivus*, must be more or less contemporary with Tomb S. Once decorated with fine plaster ornaments, most of which are lost today, it was considerably damaged, in 1626, by the work on the foundation of Bernini's baldacchino. This is the exact spot where, in that year, the tomb of the bon vivant *Flavius Agricola* was found, with the inscription[2] that, as I have said, aroused such a scandal that the sarcophagus itself was thrown into the Tiber. For us, Tomb R has a special interest since its eastern outer wall bears an important Christian graffito.[3]

On the same side of the *clivus*, Tomb R abuts Tomb R[1], which was, however, constructed later. Still it can be established that this tomb is also earlier than the Red Wall. In Tomb R[1] a tile was found with a seal of the same type as that which dated the tiles of the gutter (about 146 to 161 A.D.) In brief, R[1] can probably be dated between about 150 and 160.

Even more recent than R[1] is the Tomb Q, which could be better described as a burial area consisting of a series of

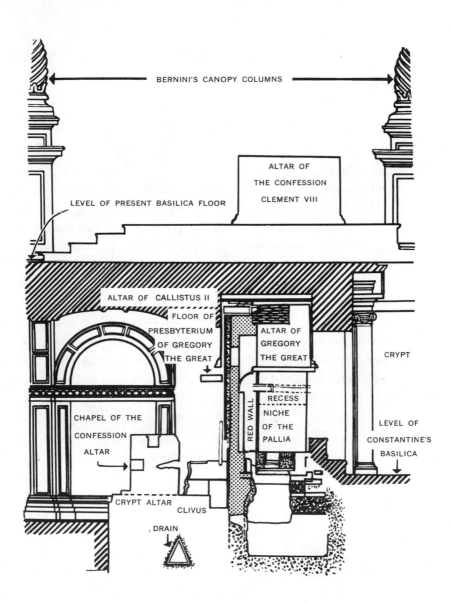

FIG. 25. Diagram of area under the Papal Altar.

tombs around an open courtyard. Still, Tomb Q seems to belong to a time not much later than the previously mentioned tombs.

These are, in brief, the structures surrounding Field P. But in Field P itself, what did the excavators find?

Field P was full of burial tombs. Some of these were brought to light during the 1939-1949 excavations; others, in much greater numbers, by the successive excavations of the years 1955-1957. These tombs are generally quite modest, situated in the bare ground with little or no protection. Some of them are certainly older than the Red Wall, i.e., as I have explained, before about 160 A.D. One of these is the tomb indicated by the excavators with the Greek letter *gamma* (γ): a child's tomb which extends partly under the Red Wall, which shows that it must be older than the wall. A precious clue to establish its date comes from a seal pressed into one of the tiles covering it. The seal is dated by scholars at the beginning of the second century (about 115-123),[4] and it is quite probable that the tomb is not much later than this date. Tomb *gamma* is also interesting because one of its walls contains a terra cotta tube through which libations were poured from the outside in honor of the deceased. This is essentially a pagan custom, but it was adopted for a while by some Christians.

Other tombs in Field P can be dated earlier than the Red Wall. They are usually designated by the Greek letters *eta* (η) and *theta* (ϑ). The first is certainly more ancient than the Red Wall since the two little columns of St. Peter's Memorial are placed upon it, and this monument, as I shall explain in a moment, is contemporary with the Red Wall. The second of these tombs (*theta*) is under Tomb *eta* and so, necessarily, earlier. In addition, Tomb *theta* has, on one of its tiles, a seal that can be dated in the time of the Emperor Vespasian (69-79). This seal was already discussed in the chapter on the

Fig. 26. Reconstruction of the shrine in the Red Wall.

Vatican in antiquity;[5] and the fact that this tomb belongs to the first century is unquestionable. In addition, the existence of first-century tombs in this part of the Vatican necropolis is confirmed, as I have said,[6] by other documents, particularly by a lamp that can be dated with certainty in the first century, found with other funeral material from the same period in the immediate vicinity of Tomb *theta*.

All these tombs of Field P are, for us, anonymous, since none of them has preserved an epigraph in which the name of the deceased is indicated. But it is quite probable that in ancient times the names (at least some of them) were carved on tombstones rising out of the ground and that these were later lost during the many vicissitudes of the region.

The most notable characteristic of Field P was a small chapel at about the middle of the Red Wall. This is the same shrine that was, as I have mentioned, enclosed in Constantine's monument, on which later the altars of Gregory the Great, Calistus II and finally Clement VIII were built. The last named is the papal altar of the present basilica.

The very position of this shrine demonstrates its supreme importance. From ancient times until the present, it has suffered much destruction and reconstruction with consequent changes in appearance. Still, the elements which remain, studied attentively by the first excavators, have allowed them to set up a very reasonable reconstruction of it. We might almost class this reconstruction as a certitude (Fig. 26). According to the reconstruction, the building has two niches, one above the other, both cut into the Red Wall. The lower niche is 0.72 meters in width, 1.40 meters in height; the upper one, about 1.10 in width, and its height uncertain. Between the two niches, a slab of travertine is inserted horizontally, jutting out, like a table, about one meter from the side of the Red Wall. It is supported by two small marble columns (Fig. 28), located in front and on either side of the lower niche. In the floor of the shrine, there is a trap door which I shall discuss later. It is important to note that the two niches were not indented into the Red Wall after its construction, but were included in its design when it was being built. This fact is established beyond question by a detailed study of technical points. We can state positively, then, that the chapel's date is the same as that of the wall, around 160 A.D.

Under the two niches which form part of the chapel, there is another, very coarse and irregular niche in the foundation of the Red Wall. Various theories have been offered to explain the nature and purpose of this niche, but none has been powerful enough to eliminate all doubt. Therefore we shall leave the question open, waiting for the day when a satisfactory answer is found. The names given to the three niches by the first excavators are N¹, N², and N³. The niche in the foundation is N¹, while N² and N³ are, respectively, the lower and upper niches in the wall itself.

Whoever built the chapel certainly intended it to mark a place of outstanding importance, to preserve a memory for transmission to future generations.

But what did the excavators find in the necropolis under the chapel. They found clear evidence of an ancient trench,

FIG. 27. Human Bones discovered under the foundation of the Red Wall. Excavations of the Vatican cemetery.

exactly parallel—and this is a point of great significance—to the Tombs *gamma* and *theta,* which (as I have already explained) date back to before the building of the Red Wall. A little wall, called m^1 by the excavators, bounded this trench on the south, separating it from the ancient Tomb *gamma;* there was probably a similar wall on the north. These walls, built apparently in the first half of the second century, correspond to the two long sides of the trench on which the chapel was built. All around, the ground was full of coins, which could be dated from the first to the fifteenth century; these were obviously thrown here by pilgrims who came from near and far to honor the Apostle. There are four first-century coins among those found by the excavators: one from the time of Augustus (43 B.C.-14 A.D.) and three of the Emperor Domitian (81-96 A.D.)

Under the foundations of the Red Wall, and exactly under the niche N^1, the excavators found a group of human bones. These bones have been given to specialists for examination and cataloguing. The delicate work, which naturally requires long time and infinite patience, is not yet finished and therefore it is too early to give any conclusions on this discovery. We can only say that in ancient times these bones were placed together under the chapel with a determined purpose of preserving them. And since this place was of exceptional importance (the very existence of the chapel shows that quite clearly) these bones must also represent something exceptional.

There can be no question (virtually all scholars admit it) that the chapel is identical with that "trophy" of Peter proudly mentioned, only a few years after its construction, by the learned Roman priest Gaius in his controversy with the heretic Proclus.[7] It is also probable that this chapel is the "Memorial of St. Peter" recorded by the *Liber Pontificalis* among the works of Pope Anacletus (*memoriam beati Petri*

FIG. 28. One of the small marble columns of the shrine (about 160 A.D.). Excavations of the Vatican necropolis.

construxit).[8] It is true that Anacletus was Pope at the end of the first century, and that this date does not (as far as we can determine) agree with the date of our chapel; but there is a very suggestive theory supported by some scholars: that in the text of the *Liber Pontificalis* there is a confusion between Anacletus and Anicetus. The latter, indeed, occupied the papal throne from 155 to 166, a period which would coincide perfectly with the age of the chapel.

Between the time of its construction (about 160) and the time when it was enclosed in Constantine's monument (about 315) the chapel underwent modifications and additions. Thus, about the middle of the third century, another wall (called G by the excavators) was built perpendicular to the Red Wall to help support it and cover a fissure just to the right of the chapel. This wall, 0.87 meters in length and 0.45 meters thick, is the same Wall G on whose northern side are incised the precious graffiti which I shall discuss in the next chapter. To build Wall G, it was necessary to shorten slightly the northern side of the travertine "table" between niches N^2 and N^3 and to shift the small marble pillar on the northern side slightly to the south. This disturbed the harmony of the chapel's structure. In compensation, it was decided to enrich the monument by covering the floor and the walls on either side of niche N^2 with marble. Next, another wall was built (Wall S) parallel to Wall G, and the inner sides of both walls (which now enclosed the chapel on its northern and southern sides) were also faced with marble. Finally, the two small columns were (or seem to have been) connected by a lattice.

Wall G is generally considered a supporting wall, built to shore up the sagging Red Wall. But this opinion may leave room for some doubt; at any rate the addition of Wall G had the undeniable purpose of stabilizing a place of special interest. This interest is also shown by a white mosaic pavement, with a green band around the circumference, which was placed upon the whole of Field P, as though to decorate the surroundings of the Apostle's Memorial with a precious covering.

In summary, we can say that those who built the Red Wall

and its chapel, about the middle of the second century, had the precise intention of marking a place sacred to the Apostle Peter. It has been rightly observed that it would have been simpler to build the chapel beside the Red Wall, instead of laboriously indenting it into the wall. This extra effort shows a desire to indicate with absolute exactitude a place that was considered more precious than any other.[9]

But what place did they wish to indicate? Since we are dealing with St. Peter and the Vatican, there can be only two possibilities: the site of the Apostle's martyrdom or that of his tomb.

Some scholars have preferred the former theory; but it is not an easy one to support. In the first place, it is absurd to imagine that in second-century Rome it would be desirable or possible to place a public monument on the spot where a condemned man had been crucified. In addition, this part of the Vatican was certainly outside of Nero's arena, where Peter probably suffered martyrdom. Finally, if the chapel had been built to mark the site of Peter's crucifixion, it would not have been necessary to calculate its location so precisely.

If we exclude the theory that the chapel marks the site of martyrdom, the only alternative is to admit that it refers to the tomb. And in fact the faithful who built it believed that Peter's tomb was precisely there; this is shown not only by their care in marking this particular place with such absolute precision, but also by other indications. These include: the funereal character of the chapel itself, which resembles other chapels of the period found in the cemetery of St. Sebastian on the Appian Way and the one on the Sacred Isle near Ostia; the sepulchral significance that Gaius certainly gave to the word "trophy" (τρόπαιον) which he used to signify this chapel sacred to Peter;[10] and, above all, a graffito carved near to the chapel itself, which—as I shall explain in the next chapter—tells us explicitly of Peter's burial in this place.[11]

The Christians who lived in Rome about the middle of the second century, therefore, were convinced that Peter's tomb was precisely here. Was this conviction actually well-founded?

Some people have simply denied the existence of Peter's tomb, thinking that it would be impossible to recognize the man's remains in the horrible mass of flesh piled up in Nero's gardens after the barbaric spectacle. But this objection has little value. It can hardly be believed that the faithful would not follow their own martyrs' dramatic and glorious actions to the very end; or that afterward they would have neglected to bury their bodies, or whatever pitiful remains could be found. Thus, in the Epistle already mentioned,[12] which Ignatius, Bishop of Antioch, wrote to the Romans while he was going toward his martyrdom (in 107 A.D., as far as we can tell) he prays that the beasts will consume his entire body "so that, after my death, I may not be a burden to anyone." This means that his friends (some of whom had already gone to Rome to witness his martyrdom) were planning—no matter what toil and danger might be involved—to gather the precious remains of the Martyr. The same must be said of Peter, more so since his body, hanging on a cross, could be much more easily watched and recovered by the faithful.

The middle of the second century was still quite close to the year (65 or, perhaps, 67 A.D.) in which Peter suffered martyrdom. With a few rare exceptions, the Apostle's contemporaries must have been dead; but there would be many still alive whose fathers had known him in person and followed the events of his death. The popular opinion of the faithful on the precise location of his tomb in the Vatican necropolis, therefore, has considerable weight.

But what do the excavations reveal on this question? I have already mentioned that the excavators found evidence of a very ancient trench under the chapel. The fact that this trench was a grave is shown by the funereal quality of the area; we have seen[13] that it already had this quality in the first century, i.e., at the time of the Apostle. More confirmation comes from a trap door in the floor of the Memorial. This trap door, which exists today only in its outlines, is orientated not, as might have been expected, according to the architectonic lines of the Memorial, but according to the lines of the trench underneath. The trench, in turn, is orientated exactly like the ancient tombs *theta* and *gamma*. This shows—it is hard to deny it—that the trench was considered very important by those who built the Memorial, and also that it was a grave.

There is nothing in archaeology, nor in logic, to make us deny the existence of Peter's tomb under the chapel in the Red Wall.

But why, the question arises, was the presumptive grave under the chapel found largely destroyed, and why was a small deposit of bones found, instead, under niche N^1? The answer to this question is that from the first century on this area underwent various disturbances: first of all in the second century for the construction of rich mausolea and of the Red Wall; later, about the middle of the third century, for the construction of Wall G. Theoretically, it can be admitted that, in the course of the works I have mentioned, it was considered appropriate to bring together, under the Red Wall's foundation, the bones which had been found in the immediate vicinity.

In this case, it is possible that at least some of these remains are relics of St. Peter.

V

———

THE TESTIMONY OF THE
INSCRIPTIONS

IN STUDYING THE PROBLEM of St. Peter's tomb, we find a third voice, that of the epigraphs, joining in the eloquent testimony of ancient authors and excavations. It is a voice that we must hear with the greatest attention, since the epigraphs are usually precious witnesses bringing us the direct, live echo of past events. In this case, we are dealing with epigraphs written by the faithful in ancient times on various walls of the Vatican necropolis. Almost all of them belong to the category which scholars call "graffiti": that is, epigraphs scratched on a suitable surface with a pointed instrument.

There are three groups of graffiti in the immediate vicinity of the Apostle's Memorial: (a) those on Wall G, (b) on the Red Wall, and (c) on Tomb R. To these may be added a group of inscriptions (d) written with red lead and charcoal in a niche of the Valerii tomb about twenty meters away from the Memorial.

A. *The Graffiti on Wall G*

Wall G, which has already been discussed,[1] stands about six meters underneath the papal altar. When the Pope is facing the people during the celebration of Mass, this wall is on his left, that is, on the Gospel side. The wall is 0.87 meters in length, 0.45 meters thick and 0.47 meters high. This height is not, however, its original dimension; the top of the wall was cut off in the time of Constantine for the construction of the monument in honor of St. Peter.[2] As I have already mentioned, it leans perpendicularly on the Red Wall,[3] and was built about 250 A.D. to stabilize in some way an area that was thought worthy of particular respect. Later—apparently about 315[4]—it was enclosed within Constantine's monument.

Into the thickness of Wall G, a strange quadrangular repository is set, 0.77 meters long, 0.29 meters deep and 0.31 meters high, lined with marble. This repository contained some bones, remains of some precious cloth with thread of gold woven in, pieces of ancient glass, small silver nets (perhaps used for ornaments) and coins. Scholars have disagreed considerably on this material and there have been some rather bold conjectures. Among other opinions, for example, there is one that holds that during the time of Constantine the remains of St. Peter himself were put in this container, after their return to the Vatican from a stay (which many consider proved) at the shrine *in Catacumbas* on the Appian Way.[5] The more probable opinion, at present, seems to be that the mysterious repository was made in the time of Constantine when the monument was built in honor of St. Peter, and that it was used to hold various remains found in the vicinity. Rightly or not, these remains were apparently considered worthy of being kept in a sacred place.

Wall G, built, as I have said, about 250 A.D., was decorated on its northern side with a simple pictorial motif. The part of the wall still preserved shows a zone of red between two azure borders. For some time, the wall remained intact, then it began to be covered with graffiti. Apparently this began near the end of the third century; and the custom of writing on the wall continued until it was enclosed in Constantine's monument, about 315 A.D. As we shall see, some of the graffiti are certainly later than the autumn of 312.

But now let us glance at the inscribed section of Wall G. The first reaction to it might be one of dismay. There is a regular forest of lines, running in all directions, pursuing and running over each other. Only here and there are a few letters or, occasionally, a few short lines of letters, clearly legible.

In itself, this throng of inscriptions already tells us something important: that we are in a place much visited and venerated by the faithful. This type of evidence can be found at pagan as well as Christian shrines, in antiquity and also in our own time. Limiting ourselves to Christian antiquity, we might mention that in the Roman catacombs the walls near places where martyrs' bodies rest are usually covered with inscriptions. Thus, there are many epigraphs in the catacomb of St. Callistus on the Appian Way, near the crypt where the bodies of ancient martyr-popes lie; the same phenomenon is found in the catacomb of Priscilla on the Via Salaria near the tomb of the martyr Crescentio and in the cemetery of SS. Peter and Marcellinus on the Via Casilina near the resting places of those heroes of the Faith. All these writings belong to the faithful who, close to the martyrs' remains, wished to leave a memorial of themselves or, more often, of their deceased friends and relatives. Usually they consist of the names of persons, accompanied by a wish for salvation in the next world; simple and moving expressions of souls raising themselves toward God and, in the memory of the martyrs, asking

God to grant peace to the dear spirits that have left this world.

The inscriptions covering Wall G in the Vatican necropolis are also of this kind. But there is something that distinguishes them from inscriptions in other Christian cemeteries. In the first place, they are much more crowded than usual, and this crowding does not merely reflect the lack of space but also, without doubt, the exceptional importance the faithful attribute to this spot. Another meaningful characteristic is their very intense use of a cryptographic system. The discovery of this cryptography, used by the faithful in the place sacred to the Apostle to express the deepest feelings of their hearts, represents—in my opinion—one of the most conspicuous benefits from my long work in the excavations under St. Peter's.

But this cryptography is also found outside the Vatican. The same keys that unlocked the "code" on Wall G also unlock the hidden meaning of other inscriptions in and out of Rome. In these inscriptions, students of Christian archaeology had already noted certain irregularities but had not considered them very important, explaining them as whims or errors on the part of those who had written the texts. But now it is possible to show that the irregularities were intentional, part of the cryptographic system whose existence is revealed to us by the graffiti on Wall G.

So far as I have been able to determine in my researches up to now, the use of this cryptography appears in laudatory epigraphs, particularly on tombs, between the second and sixth centuries. It was used in Rome and outside of Rome, even in regions far from Italy. But the Roman documents are by far the most numerous, so much so that one is led to consider this a phenomenon which originated in Rome and then spread, more or less rapidly, to other parts of the Empire. Still it is possible that, as research progresses, many other examples may be found outside the City, and traces of its survival may even be observed in the Middle Ages.

But before explaining this cryptographic system, it would be well to inquire why the early Christians used it. What purpose was served by this secret and conventional mode of expressing the secrets of the Faith? The many brutal persecutions suffered by followers of Christ, from the time of Nero onward, leap immediately to mind; and certainly it is easy to see why the faithful would want to hide their identity and the most intimate, precious concepts of their Faith from the enemy. But if the historic fact of persecution had some importance in the development of this unique cryptography, it was certainly not its cause. The first roots of the phenomenon must rather be sought in two tastes which the ancient Christians had in common with the pagans of their time: a taste for artifice and a propensity toward mystery. These are two very ancient qualities. The first originated in the classical world some centuries before Christ and the second is directly connected with human nature, which finds an air of mystery most favorable for thinking of God and hearing His voice. This irrepressible thirst for the divine is precisely what men hoped to satisfy in the foundation of the famous mystery religions which, having flourished in Greece and other parts of the Eastern Mediterranean, were transplanted to Rome where they found enthusiastic adherents during the late republican and early imperial eras. But though they shared these tendencies with the pagans, the Christians made them their own, infusing in them the spirit of the new Faith.

The religious importance and also the practical value attributed by Christianity to the element of mystery can be seen, if we look closely, in the Gospels, where Christ often uses the symbolic veil of parables to hide His highest teachings. This tendency grew stronger, little by little, and finally gave birth, from the third to fifth centuries, to the so-called *disciplina arcani* (a term which did not come into use until the seventeenth century). This is the system set up by the Church to keep certain truths of the Faith and certain liturgical actions (particularly those of Baptism and the Eucharist) hidden from the eyes of the uninitiated, under a veil of reserve and silence, since it was believed that a gradual learning was more useful than a flash of revelation. As we approach the fourth century, the desire for secrecy becomes more lively and takes a particular form. The beauty of mystery begins to be enjoyed in itself, and the idea arises that veils of secrecy give nobility to the thoughts and actions they cover. This idea reaches its full development about the end of the fourth and beginning of the fifth century. It is shown clearly by the great Doctor of the Church, St. Augustine, who more than once in his writings praises the providential obscurity of the Bible and, at the same time, the veils with which the Church conceals the most important and delicate actions of its liturgy.

This is the spiritual climate in which the cryptographic system began and developed. As I have mentioned, it was widely used in Rome from the third to the fifth century and it is found in full bloom in the graffiti of Wall G. Its purpose was not only to give the Christians freedom to express their feeling during times of persecution, but also that of bringing, by its own power, comfort to the faithful. The one who wrote must have felt the joy of expressing the highest ideas of the Faith in a brief and effective form. The reader certainly felt an equal joy, recognizing, hidden in these epigraphs, the divine truth which sustained and gave hope to his life. When the text was written on a tomb, there was also the desire to weave thoughts of salvation, and wishes for eternal joy, secretly into the names and phrases.

Now it is time to explain the keys to this cryptographic system. They are very simple keys, and their very simplicity proves that they are authentic. They can be reduced essentially to three:

A. the attribution of a symbolic value to almost every letter of the alphabet;

B. the joining of certain letters through added signs of union, to express mystic concepts;

C. the transfiguration of certain letters into others, or into Christian symbols, to show several thoughts simultaneously.

The most frequent phenomenon is the first: that of alphabetical symbolism. Let us stop here for a moment to look at it more closely. In itself, it is nothing new. Everyone knows, at least, the meaning of "beginning" and "end" attributed by Christians—from the time of the Gospels until our own—to the Greek letters *alpha* and *omega*. In the *Apocalypse,* written at the end of the first century, these two letters, the first and the last in the Greek alphabet, are applied sometimes to God and sometimes to Christ, to say that the Supreme Being and the Son who is identified with Him are the beginning and the end of created things. It is also known, from a Christian writer who lived in Egypt at the end of the first and beginning of the second century,[6] that the ancient Christians saw in the Greek letter *tau* (T) a symbol of the Cross; evidently because this letter resembles the Cross in its form, and also because it is derived from a Semitic sign (the taw) which the ancient Hebrews considered lucky. The letter *ypsilon,* which the pagan sect of Pythagoreans considered very important, was also given special values by the early Christians, its significance for them (as also, perhaps for the Pythagoreans) rising from the fact that it was the beginning of the word ὑγίεια (*hygieia*) meaning "health." (In the Greek, the "h" is a simple breathing mark, making the ypsilon the first letter of the word.)

All these meanings have long been recognized, but it is difficult today to imagine how far the Christians had gone on the road of alphabetical symbolism. The inscriptions on Wall G and other Christian epigraphs of the first centuries show that the faithful finally came to attribute a symbolic value to many letters of the alphabet; usually to the initial letters of favorite words. Thus, to mention a few examples, E took on the meaning of *Eden*, N (because it was the beginning of the Greek *nika*) that of "victory," the R that of "resurrection" (from the Latin *resurrectio*), and S that of "health" (from the Latin *salus*), the double V (W) signified, as it does today, a wish for life (*vivas* or *vivatis*—"may you live").

Very important is the letter A, which keeps its original meaning of "beginning" in the formula AΩ (or in Latin letters AO) and in other cases takes the meaning of "life" or "Christ-life." And it is not hard to understand the reason. The idea of "beginning" could lead naturally to that of "beginning of eternal life" and later to that of "life in the absolute sense," i.e., "Christ-life," since the Redeemer is, for Christians, life *par excellence*. Thus we should not be surprised to read, on Wall G and elsewhere, the wish IN A (or I A) with the same meaning as IN ☧ (*in Christo*), and to find the well-known formula AO sometimes inverted into OA, with the evident purpose of wishing the soul safe passage "from the end to the beginning," that is, from the end of human life to the beginning of heavenly life, which is equivalent to Life in the absolute sense, or Christ. Wall G also presents frequent groups of three A's, or three V's or three N's, variously arranged. It is an ingenious way to express the concept of the Holy Trinity. In the first two cases, the three A's or the three V's evidently indicate the Trinity in its aspect of life, while the three N's are intended to exalt the eternal victory of the triune God.

The second phenomenon of this religious cryptography concerns adjoining or connected letters. The alphabetical signs are intentionally placed side by side or joined together by added lines to associate two or more concepts. The third phenomenon, that of transfiguration, consists in transforming one letter into another or into a symbol of special significance as, for example, the monogram of Christ (X or ⚹ or ☧) to enrich the epigraph with new mystical values.

Before examining closely some of the graffiti on Wall G, it seems appropriate to consider briefly some phenomena of mystical cryptography in Roman inscriptions outside the Vatican necropolis.

I choose a few examples out of many which I have used in the first volume of my recent publication *I graffiti sotto la Confessione di San Pietro in Vaticano*.

1. A tombstone found in the cemetery of Sant' Ermete on the Via Salaria, now kept in the Lateran Museum (Fig. 29), bears a wife's dedication to her dead husband named Renatus: RENATO COIVGI BENEMEREN(TI) ("to Renatus, an excellent husband"). Looking at this stone, one immediately notices a strange detail: from the vertical stroke of the T in *Renato* three small parallel lines extend to the right. Why this addition? The three lines, added to the T, produce a combination of T and E. Since the T means "Cross" and the E "Eden" (or Paradise), the union of the two letters also represents the union of the Cross to Paradise, since the Cross is the necessary condition for reaching heavenly joy. The group TE is between the letters A and O, which signify Christ as the Beginning (A) and the End (O equals *omega*) of the universe. The meaning, then, was that in Christ, beginning and end (AO), it is possible, thanks to the Cross (T) to reach Paradise (E). Applied to the deceased, this naturally becomes a prayer for eternal happiness.

2. On a small piece of marble, coming from an unknown location in Rome and now kept in the Lapidary of the Vatican Museums (Fig. 30), we find, carved on a single line: a large vase, an M, a dove, and finally the letters RA. The vase

FIG. 29. Epitaph of *Renatus*. Rome, Lateran Museum (from the cemetery of Sant 'Ermete).

—it is already well established—is a symbol of eternal refreshment, i.e., of heavenly life, and so also of Christ, life of the faithful; the dove usually signifies the soul of the deceased. But what is the M? As we shall see, the graffiti of Wall G demonstrate with certitude that M signified the name of Mary. And now everything becomes clear: the soul (dove) turns toward Mary and toward the mystical vase to express the idea that through Mary we reach Life, i.e., Christ; the letters RA, to the right of the little scene, are closely united and seem to sum up the scene itself. R and A signify "resurrection" and "life" and recall to our minds the famous words of St. John's Gospel in which Christ, just before the resurrection of Lazarus, says of Himself: "I am the Resurrection and the Life."

3. A gravestone in the cemetery of St. Callistus (Fig. 31) has an inscription dedicated to the exorcist *Celer* (the exorcist, it is well-known, had the function of driving away evil spirits through prayer) and his wife: CELERI EXORC(ISTAE) CVM COMPARE SVA IN PACE ("to Celer the exorcist, with his companion, in peace"). The upper right corner of this stone gives us a significant example of mystic

FIG. 30. Christian epitaph. Lapidary of the Vatican Museums.

cryptography. The E, meaning "Eden," is decorated with special care by a branch which crosses it and which—one might say—is intended to represent ideographically the joys of the heavenly Garden. The M of *cum* is strangely transfigured into a combination of M and A. Why? Notice that above the M, on the preceding line, there is a letter X. This (as is well known) represents Christ, being the Greek initial of the Redeemer's name (χριστός). Now, it was precisely the nearness of an M to the symbol of Christ that suggested the idea of expressing the comforting association of the names of Christ and Mary. The M, by itself, could indicate the name of the Virgin. But to make this name stand out more clearly, the M was transformed into a combination of M and A, i.e., the two letters which are the first and the last in MARIA and represent in abbreviation the name of the Mother of God. The sign ﰃ, which can still be found on altars dedicated to the Madonna and other sacred objects is precisely the same. The hidden meaning of the epigraph in St. Callistus is therefore the wish that the deceased may reach Paradise (E) through the protection of Christ (X) and Mary (ﰃ).

4. A graceful little stone in the cemetery of St. Agnes on the Via Nomentana (Fig. 32) offers us a very clear specimen of cryptography. Only the lower right corner of the piece of marble is preserved; the rest of the stone has broken off. We find a large A, certainly the end of a woman's name (that of

Fig. 31. Epitaph of the exorcist *Celer*. Rome, cemetery of St. Callistus.

the deceased) and, on the line below, two vertical strokes which undoubtedly belong to the number of years, months or days lived by the deceased. At right, completely isolated, is an N, whose right stroke extends strangely between the feet of a bird. The bird holds a bunch of grapes in its beak and extends it toward the A of the first line. Recalling that the N, beginning of *nika*, was used symbolically by Christians to express the idea of "victory," it is easy to find the hidden meaning of the little scene. The soul, represented by the bird, stands upon victory (N) to reach life (A). In other words, the wish is expressed that the deceased may enter victoriously into eternal life.

To this wish is added the meaningful idea represented by the bunch of grapes which the bird holds in his beak. The grape had a well-known and deep symbolic value for Christians; it indicated the joys of the other world, and at the same time, it often referred to the sacrament of the Eucharist which the faithful took as an anticipation and a guarantee of

FIG. 32. Christian epitaph. Rome, cemetery of St. Agnes.

FIG. 33. Epitaph of *Ursa*. Urbino, Duke's Palace (taken from Rome).

the joys of Paradise. In this case, the meaning might be that the soul, for which victory and life were invoked, had departed to the heavenly kingdom prepared and nourished on this earth by the comforts of the Eucharist.

5. A tomb inscription, found some time ago in a Roman catacomb and now kept at Urbino in the Museum of the Ducal Palace (Fig. 33), referred to a Christian woman named *Ursa*. The epitaph is very brief: VRSES SEP(VLCRVM) ("Ursa's tomb"). The Greek genetive *Urses* instead of *Ursae* and the abbreviation *sep.* for sepulcrum are normal. But strange and very worthy of note is the disposition of the name VRSES. The V and the R are together, united with each other, and a large space separates them from the remaining letters SES. Exactly under the group VR a monogram of Christ (☧) is carved. The symbolic meaning is transparent. The intention is to state that Christ (☧) is the Life and Resurrection (VR); a thought which, applied to the deceased *Ursa*, corresponds to a wish that she may live and rise in Christ.

Now let us consider the graffiti on Wall G.

The first excavators of the Vatican necropolis, not recog-

Fig. 34. Christian epitaph. Rome, cemetery of Ciriaca.

nizing the cryptographic system on this wall, could read and understand only a very small part of its inscriptions. They said that all they could find there was the name of Christ, expressed by the sign (✗), but not that of Peter. This absence of the Apostle's name, precisely in the place which more than any other should be sacred to him, naturally seemed very strange. Some scholars tried to explain it with more or less complicated reasoning, while others found it a sufficient reason to deny flatly the presence of the Apostle's tomb. In reality, the Apostle's name occurs more than once on Wall G. But it is not written out completely, rather it is abbreviated to P or PE or PET.

Peter's name is also expressed on Wall G and in other epigraphic documents by a characteristic sign: ᛒ or ᛒ or ᛒ. This sign links the letters P and E, initials of the name *Petrus,* and, at the same time, reproduces the very significant form of a key.

The presence of this symbol on Wall G, with the evident meaning of *Petrus,* permits us to solve an age-old riddle which has irritated scholars since the eighteenth century. Al-

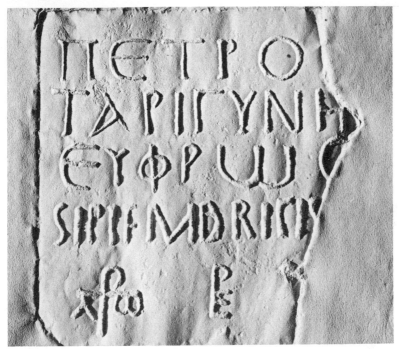

FIG. 35. Christian epitaph. Rome, cemetery of Ciriaca.

though many examples of the symbol were known, almost all of them in Roman documents datable between the fourth and fifth centuries, its meaning had never been determined. It appeared on sepulchral epigraphs, usually next to the symbol of Christ (Figs. 34, 35), on public inscriptions (such as the epigraph commemorating a restoration of the Colosseum), on mosaics, facets of rings, game boards, domestic objects of various kinds and, in particular, on medals of Roman coinage which have been found throughout the Empire.

With the discovery of the symbol's meaning, we now have an idea of the immense popularity enjoyed by Peter during the early centuries of the Church. The widespread use of Peter's name on profane objects such as rings and gaming tables might seem strange, but the difficulty vanishes when

Fig. 36. Christian epitaph. Museum of Naples (taken from Rome).

we consider that, like the symbol of Christ, that of Peter took on an added value with the passage of years: that of a charm for good luck and protection. It is also very probable that, in Peter's case, still another new meaning was added: that of a symbol of Rome. The presence of Peter's symbol on profane objects is therefore fully explainable.

The protective value was also increased by the resemblance of the abbreviation to the form of a key, a very popular symbol of good luck from ancient times to the present. Of course in Peter's case the key also has another special significance: it is an allusion to the "keys of the kingdom of heaven" which Christ conferred on the Chief of the Apostles as a sign of his authority to represent the Lord on earth and to guide the faithful to eternal salvation. The famous words of the Gospel of St. Matthew,[7] in which Christ declares that he intends to give Peter the symbolic keys, very soon gave him the position of heavenly gatekeeper in the popular imagination.

This idea, or more precisely the hope that the gatekeeper will open the gates of Paradise for the deceased, can be traced in a key carved, as a good luck symbol, at the beginning of a Christian epitaph taken from one of the catacombs and now preserved in the Museum of Naples (Fig. 36).

On Wall G a characteristic formula appears frequently: AP or APE or APET. In this formula we can easily recognize the name of Peter (P, PE, PET), preceded by the preposition *ad,* which in Latin is often reduced to a simple *a.* The existence of the formula *ad Petrum* is also confirmed by analogous formulas such as *ad Crescentionem, ad Hippolytum,* etc. With these expressions, the faithful were accustomed to express the nearness of the deceased to the tombs of the martyrs (Crescentio, Hippolytus, and so forth). This refers to the idea, widespread among the early Christians, that the deceased buried near the remains of martyrs would obtain from this nearness a guarantee of eternal salvation. But when it refers to Peter, the formula *ad Petrum* seems also to have taken on a further votive meaning: that of nearness to Peter in Paradise.

Besides Peter's name, Wall G naturally presents that of Christ. This usually occurs in the abbreviations X or ✦ or ✳ (Christus Iesus) or (in only one case) the abbreviation ₽. It often appears intimately united to the sign of Peter. This union, as can easily be seen, has a profound meaning, since it reflects the intimate link between Christ and Peter in the hearts of the faithful and gives us a very clear proof of the immense importance attributed to Peter as legitimate Vicar of the Redeemer. It even reached a point where some epithets that originally belonged to Christ alone (such as *lux et dux*) were extended to Peter.

But near to the names of Christ and Peter Wall G also offers, several times, that of Mary; this is another great surprise reserved for us by the precious wall. The name of the

Mother of God is sometimes expressed by a simple M, some-times by the syllable MA (which might be the first syllable of the name, or, better, its contraction: Ma(ria) or M(ari)a); but one graffito, which we shall examine in a moment, for-tunately presents it complete: MARIA, and thus permitting us to recognize the Virgin's name also where it appears in the abbreviated forms M or MA.

I have already mentioned that Wall G was built around 250 A.D. and that writing on it began only several decades later; in any case the graffiti are earlier than the monument built by Constantine in honor of the Apostle, since Wall G was enclosed in that construction and—at least on its in-scribed side—remained invisible and inaccessible until the excavations brought it back to light. I have also explained that Constantine's monument seems to be no later than the year 315.[8] Therefore we can assign our graffiti, approximately, to the years between 290 and 315 A.D. The last graffiti, as we shall see, refer to the battle of Constantine against Maxentius near the Milvian Bridge (October 28, 312). This date is in complete harmony with the character of the graffiti carved on the wall, that is, with the religious cryptography which dis-tinguishes them, since the maximum development of the *disciplina arcani* was between the end of the third and the beginning of the fourth century.

And now it is time to examine directly some of the graffiti on Wall G. I must limit myself here to a necessarily small selection, which however, I hope, will be sufficient to give an idea of this document and of its historic and religious im-portance. Passing over many graffiti which are nevertheless noteworthy from many points of view, I think it would be ap-propriate to call attention to some of those that speak of the Apostle and to those, of great historic interest, which allude to Constantine and his victory.

On the upper part of Wall G, toward the left, there is a

graffito written in large and prominent letters: ⳨ LEONIA. (Plates IV, V.)

It is the name of a dead woman, preceded by the mono-gram of Christ. But this is only what we might call the basic graffito. With appropriate additions it became a true em-broidery of thoughts expressing the faith of the survivors and their hope that this soul might enjoy the prize of eternal blessedness. Let us observe some of the details of this pious embroidery.

The ⳨ which precedes the name of the deceased was en-riched with new values. At its upper extremity a line was drawn to unite the symbol of Christ (⳨) with that of the Cross (T) (Plates IV, IX).

This line then serves as the basis of an E which lies almost flat on top of the P in the ⳨ . (Plates IV, IX.)

Some ancient Roman Christian inscriptions show that the P in ☧ could have the Latin meaning of *pi* besides its original Greek meaning of *rho*. For example, seals found in the catacomb of St. Agnes bear a ☧ whose P functions simultaneously as *rho* and *pi*. Note that this is the case with the Latin *pi* in the word SPES from the phrase *Spes Dei* (Fig. 37).

Fɪɢ. 37. Christian seal. Rome, cemetery of St. Agnes.

In the ☧ of our wall inscription we can also find the double value of *rho* and *pi* and recognize the union of Christ's sign with that of Peter (PE). (Plates IV, IX.)

In addition, by using the vertical line of the ☧ and the line added above, and carving three more lines, a group of three A's was produced, one inside the other. As I have said, this is a symbol of the Holy Trinity, AAA (Plates IV, IX).

Finally, the addition of a small line at the upper end of one of the diagonal strokes of the ☧ made it possible to form an N with the right stroke very prolonged (a sign which corresponds to the syllable NI in Latin palaeography). A C was added at the left of the upper vertical line in the ☧, and thus the word NICA (Greek *nika*) was formed to serve as a cry of victory. (Plates IV, IX.)

This ingenious embroidery therefore became a cry of victory directed at Christ and Peter, mingled with thoughts of the Cross of salvation and the Holy Trinity.

Next, the inscription I VIVIS TV is written across the precious ☧ (Plates IV, IX)

and enriched by the addition W APET (Plates IV, IX)

which forms the phrase *i(n) vivis tu v(i)v(e) a(d) Pet(rum)*: the wish that the deceased may be among those "living" souls which enjoy the life of the next world close to Peter ("may you live among the living close to Peter").

The same wish I VIVIS AP ‖ (Plate IV)

with the E expressed, this time, in the cursive form by two parallel lines (‖), can be seen, written apparently by the same hand, a bit lower.

The letters of the name LEONIA were next elaborated in a remarkable way to express religious concepts and good wishes. For example, the L was transfigured into the sign of Peter ℔ (Plate IV) for the purpose of inscribing the helpful sign of the Apostle in the name of the deceased. The final A was transformed into a small treasure chest of precious thoughts. First, on the right stroke, two more A's were erected to present the trinitarian concept AAA (Plates V, X)

and to the left of the letter, above it, was written the preposition IN, with the evident purpose of expressing the wish for life in the threefold God: IN AAA (Plates V, X).

In addition, the second of the three A's was enriched with the symbol of Christ ✗ (Plates V, X)

very appropriately, since Christ is the second Person of the Holy Trinity. The ☧, in turn, was then enriched with three more small A's (Plates V, X).

Finally, on either side of the ☧ were written the letters A and P (Plates V, X)

signifying the wish for life close to Peter (a(d) P(etrum)).

Now let us consider a graffito located near the center of the wall. The inscription consists in the names of four dead persons written on two lines and then repeated all together on a third line: VENEROSA VEA / VERV BONIFATIA / VERVS BONIFATIA VENEROSA VEA (Plates V, VI, VII).

VENEROSAVEA
VERVBONIFATIA

VERVSBONIFATIAVENEROSAVEA

Here, too, the names of the deceased were elaborated with ingenious embroidery to express many thoughts and wishes. Let us examine a few of them.

Beginning at the bottom and moving upward, we notice a ☧ set up directly above the second A of *Bonifatia* on the third line; a ☧ written in such a way that it was located between three A's (besides the A on which it stands, the two A's of *Bonifatia* on the second line). (Plates VI, VII, XI.)

A sign of union binds this ☧ to the T of *Bonifatia* on the second line, undoubtedly to express the idea that Christ is closely associated with the Cross (T) (Plates VI, VII, XI).

As in the *Leonia* graffito, the ☧ here is also flanked by A and P, signifying the wish for life close to Peter.

VE NE ROSAVEA
VERVBONIFATIA

VE RVSBONIFATIAVENEROSAVEA

Another link binds together the first A of *Bonifatia* on the second line and the O of *Venerosa* on the first line, obviously to produce the formula AO signifying God (or Christ) beginning and end of the universe. (Plates VI, VII, XI.)

VE NE ROSAVEA
VERVBONIFATIA

VE RVSBONIFATIAVENEROSAVEA

There is also a second ⳨ linked with an A (Plates VI, VII, XI)

written above the O and A of *Venerosa* on the first line. (Plates VI, VII, XI.)

This expresses the concept that through "Christ-life" (☧ A) one can pass from death to life (O A).

But the writer of the graffito was not yet satisfied. Adding an E to the base of the ☧ and using the P as both *rho* and *pi*, he managed to produce the customary union of Christ's name (☧) with that of Peter (PE). (Plates VI, VII, XI.)

At the top of the ✶ was written (perhaps by another hand) the cry of victory NICA (the Greek *nika*) (Plates VI, VII, XI)

and, writing an M over the ✶ and taking advantage of the A in *nica*, the entire name of Mary was carved (Plates VI, VII, XI).

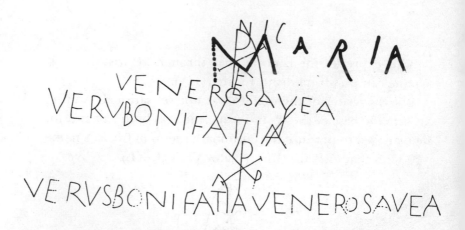

Christ, Peter and Mary are therefore linked together, as they are also in other parts of Wall G, in the same cry of victory.

The few examples already introduced are sufficient to give an idea of the spiritual richness on the inscribed surface of Wall G.

I have mentioned the fact that among the other graffiti

there are some alluding to the Emperor Constantine and to his victory over Maxentius which marks, in the history of the Church, the beginning of peace after a. long period of persecution and struggles. There are two of these inscriptions, the first carved in the upper left corner of the wall, the second about halfway up the wall near the right end.

The first of these graffiti is to the right of the ☧ preceding the name of the deceased *Leonia,* and it was undoubtedly written with reference to that sign. The inscription reads: HOC VIN(CE) (Plates IV, IX).

The expression *hoc vince* ("with this, conquer") next to the sign of the Redeemer can only be a reference to the famous vision of Constantine on the eve of the battle with Maxentius near the Milvian Bridge, October 28, 312. Some years after the battle, at least later than 325, Eusebius, Bishop of Caesarea in Palestine, heard the story of this memorable event from the lips of Constantine himself. He refers to it in his Life of Constantine,[9] and states that the Emperor swore he was telling the whole truth and nothing but the truth.

This is what Eusebius wrote: "He said that with his own eyes, during the afternoon, while the day was already fading, he had seen a shining Cross in the sky, more brilliant than the sun, accompanied by the words: 'with this, conquer.' He remained stunned by the vision, and so did all the army following him in the expedition, which had also seen the miracle." During the night of this same day, Constantine said he saw Christ Himself in a dream, bearing the same sign of salvation that had already appeared brilliantly in the sky. Eusebius does not specify that the expedition during which the miracle occurred was the one by the Milvian Bridge. But confirmation of this fact comes to us from the words of a contemporary Roman writer, Lactantius, in a brief work about the deaths of persecutors (*De mortibus persecutorum*). Lactantius does not mention the heavenly vision and the phrase *hoc vince,* but he does tell of the apparition of Christ to the Emperor in a dream and states explicitly that Constantine was then near the Milvian Bridge, on the eve of the battle with Maxentius.[10]

Eusebius' story of the vision, with the "sign of the Cross" accompanied by the words "with this, conquer" has been questioned by some scholars, who described it as either an invention by Eusebius or a passage added to his work in later times. There was even a theory that denied Eusebius' authorship of the *Life of Constantine,* stating that this work must be at least a century later than the time of the Bishop of Caesarea.

Now the graffito on Wall G has demonstrated the poor foundation of these doubts. Since it is, as I have said, certainly earlier than the construction of Constantine's monument in honor of St. Peter, i.e., about 315 A.D., the conclusion must be that the story of the miracle and the prophetic phrase were already known, at least in Rome, quite a few years before Eusebius wrote the biography of Constantine. It is also significant that the expression *hoc vince* was found on Wall G next to the ☧. This immediate proximity indicates that the miraculous sign mentioned by Eusebius must have been the ☧ and not the common sign of the Latin Cross, as some have assumed.

Everyone is free to believe or not to believe in the historic truth of Constantine's vision. But the testimony of our graffito remains beyond discussion: the news of the miracle must have been widely known in Rome by about 315 A.D., and the miraculous sign in the case must have been the ☧. The date is almost immediately after the battle by the Milvian Bridge, and it is worth noting that a fresh, living echo of the event, even the very expression which the Emperor saw glowing in the sky as a divine prediction of his victory and of the future triumph of the Church, resounds at the heart of the Vatican basilica, directly under the papal altar.

The other graffito which refers to Constantine is particularly interesting because it links a mention of Peter's tomb with mention of the Emperor.

The basic inscription which gave origin to this graffito is very simple and presents a fairly common formula. It is a wish that two dead persons, *Victor* and *Gaudentia,* may live in Christ: VICTOR GAVDENTIA VIVATIS IN ☧. (Plates VII, VIII.)

Under this graffito, another hand later wrote—or had previously written—the expression W I A (Plates VII, VIII, XII)

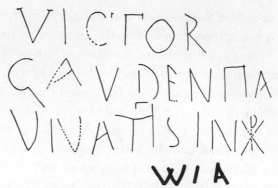

signifying, as I have already observed, *vivas* (or *vivatis*) *i(n)*
A, that is, "may you (singular or plural) live in the Life (which
means, in Christ)." If the expression was written at a later
date, it probably refers to *Victor* and *Gaudentia;* if it was
written earlier it must be considered an "anonymous" wish,
applied to deceased Christians in general and particularly to
those in the Vatican necropolis. Be that as it may, the epigraph of *Victor* and *Gaudentia* already existed when someone
decided to use the W I A as a basis for still another wish referring to these two. For this purpose, the second V of the W
was heavily rewritten and a vertical line (serving as the letter
I) was inserted after the VIVATI of the epigraph of *Victor*
and *Gaudentia,* arranged in such a way as to indicate a tran-
sition to the V I A on the line below. After the VIA, the
word SPECI was added. (Plates VII, VIII, XII, XIII.)

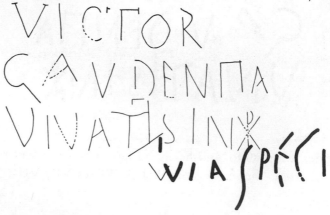

This made it possible to read two phrases simultaneously:

VIVATIS IN ☧
VIVATI I VIA SPECI

i.e., "may you live in Christ" and "may you live on the road of the crypt."

In the second phrase, the VIVATI is clearly equivalent to VIVATIS, and the I can be interpreted as IN, recalling the practice, introduced in late Latin, of dropping final consonants. The word SPECI, which is quite legible, can only be explained as the genitive singular of *specus*. True, *specus* is a fourth declension noun and we would expect the genetive to be *specus*, not *speci;* but the irregularity is only apparent since the Romans—particularly during the Imperial age— frequently confused the cases of the various declensions and often gave the endings of the second to nouns of the fourth. *Speci* is, then, the genitive of *specus,* a Latin word used to indicate a natural or artificial cave. In the language of the Christians it could mean (as various examples show) the place set apart to preserve the remains of a martyr, in other words, a crypt. And this is precisely the meaning we must give the word *speci* on Wall G. But a crypt, mentioned without any other specification in this place, could only have one meaning: the crypt of Peter, the underground grave in which, according to the firm belief of the faithful, the remains of the Apostle rested. It is very significant that, during the same period, Christ's tomb in Jerusalem was also called *specus* (or *spelunca*) and, in Greek, ἄντρον (*antron*—cave). Even in this usage, Peter had something in common with his divine Master.

As for the double wish: *vivatis in* ☧ and *vivati(s) i(n) via speci,* its meaning is easy to understand. Assuming that the tombs of *Victor* and *Gaudentia* were in the Vatican necropolis and precisely on the road which led to Peter's crypt, it is easy to understand that, in wishing the two souls life in Christ it was also found worthwhile to record the proximity of their tombs to that of the Martyr: a privilege which, in the common belief of Christians at that time, was a guarantee of eternal salvation.

The record of Constantine's victory was grafted onto the expression *in via speci* by the addition of a new and very significant word, VLTI, before SPECI (Plates VII, VIII, XII).

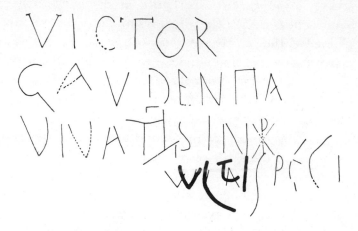

The expression *ulti speci* ("of the avenged crypt") seems obscure, but it quickly becomes clear when we consider that Constantine claimed the glory of having "avenged" Rome for the injuries suffered through the tyrant Maxentius. We are told this, for instance, in the official inscription on the Arch of Triumph which the Romans dedicated to the Emperor in 315 in memory of his victory near the Milvian Bridge: *iustis rem publicam ultus est armis* ("he avenged the state with just arms.")[11] The panegyrist Nazarius used the same verb *ulciscor* (*ulcisco*) in the discourse prepared by him for the same happy occasion.[12] At the end of the century, the Christian poet Prudentius exalted the "avenger" (*ultor*) Constantine and his "avenging" (*ultrix*) army, who had crossed the Alps to free Rome from the tyranny of Maxentius.[13]

Since the deeds of Constantine were interpreted by his contemporaries under the heading of revenge, we are able to understand the expression on our graffito: *ulti speci*. Evidently the meaning was that, just as Rome had been avenged, the Apostle's crypt, now considered a protector and practically a symbol of the City, was also vindicated.

The few graffiti examined have clearly shown that the Wall G inscriptions were not written haphazardly and without plan by occasional visitors. They are, rather, a complex embroidery of signs, traced for a clearly seen purpose, by people with an exact knowledge of the previously written graffiti. There was plainly an intention of respecting the earlier graffiti and, wherever possible, of using them to enrich the precious wall with new mystical values. This leads us to believe that not everyone had free access to this place, but only a few privileged custodians who were given the task of representing the faithful and inscribing the wall for them. Therefore we must presume that the venerated place was closed off to protect it from the sometimes excessive manifestations of popular piety. This sort of thing still happens in our own time at very popular shrines: the crowd stays outside a railing and the sacristans receive the offerings of the faithful and light candles for them before the altar, holy image, or object of special veneration.

The inscriptions on Wall G are distinguished by a deep spirituality. The thoughts of those who wrote them, animated with faith in Christian truths and hope for an eternal reward, were constantly fixed on the things of heaven. On this point, our graffiti differ radically from others found elsewhere in ancient Christian Rome and, in particular, from those under the church of St. Sebastian on the Appian Way,

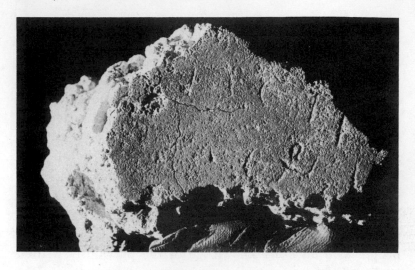

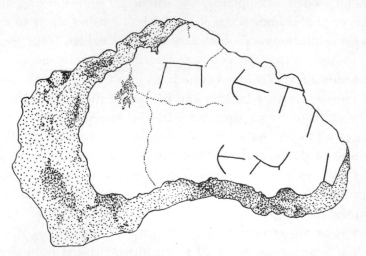

Fig. 38. Graffito of Red Wall (just after A.D. 160). Excavations of the Vatican necropolis.

a place devoted to the cult of the Apostles Peter and Paul.[14] This deep spirituality is a new and sure indication of the importance attributed by the faithful to the Apostolic Memorial in the Vaticano. Since such a fervent cult could not have risen up in a few months or even in a few years, we must conclude that it has its roots in a much earlier time.

Among the insistent aspirations to heavenly things (light, peace, salvation, Paradise, victory, life) which dominate the surface of Wall G, the figures of Christ, Peter and Mary stand out. Christ is presented as God and Son of God, participant in the Trinity, often united with the idea of the Cross and always considered as the Being in whom all Christian good is mystically summed up. Peter is often associated with Christ, and this graphic association of the two names is so close that the Apostle is considered almost one with the Redeemer.

Master and Disciple are quite often united in a single acclamation of victory. Similarly, the names of Christ and Mary are often associated, while in other cases (one of which we have examined)[15] the names of Christ, Mary and Peter are placed together and the victory of this heavenly trio is acclaimed as a motif for the encouragement of the faithful.

Summing up, we can say that Wall G contains, in synthesis, a true and proper treatise on theology; together with the memory of Peter and with historic allusions to the battle by the Milvian Bridge, it might be said to contain all the most sacred and cherished ideas of the faithful. Its location gives this treatise a particular importance, and in one sense it might almost be considered the foundation stone of the greatest Christian basilica.

B. *The Graffiti on the Red Wall*

From the numerous graffiti on Wall G, we shall now pass on to the few but no less important writings preserved on the Red Wall. These are found in a small fragment of the red plaster which once covered the wall, precisely at the place where Wall G meets the Red Wall; just above the repository which, as I have mentioned, is contained in Wall G.[16] There

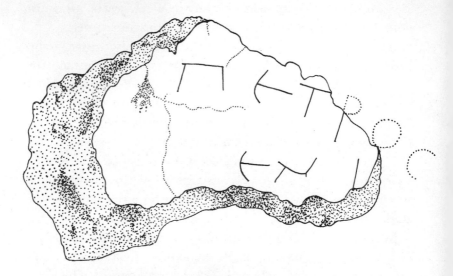

FIG. 39. Graffito of the Red Wall (reconstruction, completing the inscription). Excavations of the Vatican necropolis.

are two small graffiti, one of which has remained in its original place while the other, removed during the first excavations, is now kept in the offices of the Fabbrica di San Pietro (Building of St. Peter).

Since the Red Wall was built around 160 A.D. (a point which we established from the examination of a series of bricks with the manufacturers' seals on them)[17] and Wall G can be dated, through various archaeological and topographical data, around 250 A.D., the age of the graffiti on the Red Wall must naturally be between those two dates. One of the graffiti seems very close to the earlier date and must be considered, at least, earlier than the end of the second century.

This graffito is Greek and it is placed on two lines. There are four letters on the first line and three on the second, not very deeply carved and averaging about 0.7 centimeters in height. To the left of the inscription, the surface of the plaster shows no traces of writing; but to the right the epigraph must have continued, at least on the first line (Fig. 41).

On the first line, it is easy to recognize the beginning of Peter's name in Greek (Πέτρος). In this location, the name must naturally refer to the Apostle. This has been admitted with virtual unanimity by the scholars who have studied the graffito. On the contrary, the three letters on the second line have been interpreted in widely varying ways. Some have erroneously given importance to a slight irregularity in the plaster to the left of a vertical line, which led them to believe that the final letter of the graffito is a *delta*. Actually, it is a simple vertical line which clearly forms an *iota*.

To understand the graffito in its true significance, we must bear in mind that the first line slopes downward, as though the writer of the epigraph, finding himself in an awkward position, had used his elbow as a pivot. If we follow the broken-off line along its indicated path, it becomes evident that after two more letters it is necessary to stop to avoid crossing the second line. And to keep from running into the first line, the second must necessarily stop at the precise point where, in fact, it does end. As a result, it contains only three letters: ENI, which can only be interpreted as the Greek verb ἔνι (*eni*) often used in prose and in verse as a contraction of the form ἔνεστι. This verb means "is within" and requires a subject which is obviously to be found on the preceding line. The graffito must originally have read: Πέτρος ἔνι, and the reconstruction of the missing letters shows that this

FIG. 40. Another graffito from the Red Wall (between about 160 and about 250 A.D.). Excavations of the Vatican necropolis.

FIG. 41. Graffito from Tomb R (about 150 A.D.). Excavations of the Vatican necropolis.

reading is confirmed by the symmetrical position of ENI in relation to the first line. The meaning of the epigraph, therefore, is "Peter is within"; but this literal meaning can be explained even better. We must consider that in the vocabulary of tomb inscriptions the verb ἐνεῖναι from which ἔνι is derived is sometimes used to indicate burial, that is, the presence of a dead body "within" the tomb. This usage is particularly common in Asia Minor and corresponds exactly to a Latin verb used in the same way: *inesse*. Ἔνι (ἔνεστι) is a precise equivalent of *inest*.

If, as it seems certain, our graffito signifies "Peter is buried inside here," this throws important light on the problem of the Apostle's tomb, and it immediately becomes necessary to date the inscription as precisely as possible.

One indication comes, as I have said, from the respective dates of the Red Wall and Wall G: about 160 A.D. and about 250 A.D. The graffito was certainly done sometime between these two dates. But, even if the character of the letters were not inappropriate for the third century, the use of the Greek language would make us think rather of the second. It is well known that the earliest Christian inscriptions in Rome are written in Greek, the common language of the first followers of the new religion from the Orient. The nature of the graffito also supports this opinion. Its small, lightly inscribed letters, and its very position on the Red Wall, argue against the theory that it is a true and proper sepulchral epigraph. It is also improbable that it would be the work of a pilgrim who had come to venerate Peter's tomb. Rather, we should probably consider it a sort of notation written to mark the exact location of the tomb. Therefore the graffito would probably have been carved shortly after the Red Wall was built, changing the aspect of the area. In short, it seems to be very slightly later than the construction of the Memorial, about 160 A.D.

This brings us to a time not very distant from that in which Gaius, replying to the heretic Proclus, invited him to come to Rome and promised to show him the "trophies" of Peter and Paul respectively in the Vatican and on the Via Ostiense. I have already explained why the "trophies" mentioned by Gaius must be identified with the tombs of the Apostles.[18] Now our graffito, speaking of Peter's tomb in this area, gives full confirmation to this interpretation.

The other graffito on the Red Wall (Fig. 40), has stayed in place. It is also written in Greek letters and consists in a single line mutilated at the beginning and the end:

Among the letters still legible, we can make out the group KAIP followed by an apostrophe. This is evidently the imperative singular of the verb χαίρειν, (*Chairein*) written, as it was sometimes during the Imperial era, with a K instead of a X. Its meaning is equivalent to the Latin "salve," the English "hail." We cannot say with certainty who is the object of this greeting; but considering the place where it is found it seems probable that it was directed at the Chief of the Apostles.

C. *The Graffiti of Tomb R*

Discussing the Memorial of Peter, I have already mentioned that Tomb R is behind the Red Wall, on the other side of the *clivus,* and that it can be dated between 130 and 150.[19] The graffiti which interest us here are inscribed on the pretty brick surface which covers the eastern side of the tomb. If we look closely we are immediately impressed by the fact that the wall was a favorite surface for inscriptions for a long time. Considering that it faces the *clivus* behind the Red Wall, one is inclined to think that passers-by must have liked to linger at this spot.

Some of the graffiti seem to be meaningless, carved—one would conjecture—to pass the time: rows of vertical lines, little geometric figures and so forth. But there are others with

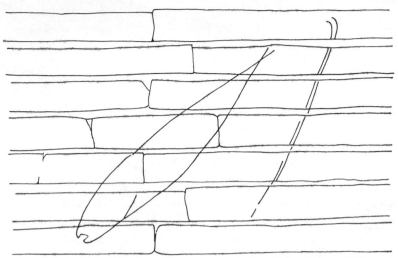

FIG. 42. Figure of a fish on the wall of Tomb R (about 150 A.D.). Excavations of the Vatican necropolis.

a very precise meaning. Among the latter there is a Greek graffito on three lines (Fig. 44):

Ἐμνήσθη Λ. Πάκκιος
Εὔτυχος
Γλύκωνος

Emnesthe L. Pakkios
Eutychos
Glykonos

that is, "Lucius Paccius Eutychus remembers Glycon." This very brief phrase had already been read by the first excavators and duly reported, but no special importance had ever been found in it. But it does have considerable significance in the study of ancient devotion to St. Peter in the Vatican.

The name Πάκκιος is simply a transliteration into Greek of the Latin family name *Paccius*. The family of the *Paccii* seems to have originated in Campania, but many members are found later in Rome and elsewhere; so it is not necessary to believe that our Lucius Paccius Eutychus was a native of Southern Italy. It seems rather (as indicated by his cognomen, Eutychus, borrowed from the Greek) that he was a freedman, given his liberty by an owner who belonged to the *gens Paccia*.

Lucius Paccius Eutychus is a completely unknown person; and the Glycon mentioned by him is equally obscure: perhaps another freedman or even a slave. But the formula of the inscription is well known and very meaningful: "so-and-so remembered so-and-so." This is one of those texts which scholars refer to with the Latin term *tituli memoriales,* that is, inscriptions intended to record the names of distant friends in places of special interest. This interest could be based on popular devotion, a fame for natural beauty or any other characteristic that would attract visitors. Sometimes the importance of a certain place would arise from its being the beginning or the end of a difficult journey.

A very large number of *tituli memoriales* have been preserved from antiquity. Most of them are pagan, but some Christian ones are also known. Usually they owe their origin to a religious sentiment and they correspond, in a way, to prayers. It is not difficult to understand that when a person prayed at a shrine reached through great effort, or when he looked at a beautiful, grandiose or unusual spectacle, when he rejoiced at having escaped a danger or worried before facing one, his thoughts would naturally turn with affection to his distant loved ones and he would wish to leave in that place a tangible record of those who had been in his mind: a record linking his own name with those of the absent ones. This ancient custom still remains, under somewhat different forms, in our own time. How many of the faithful, when they go on a pilgrimage to a holy place, write their own names and those of their loved ones on the stones, the walls or any other available surface! And we all know that in some

FIG. 43. The heads of Christ and Peter in the tomb of the Valerii (end of the third—beginning of the fourth century A.D.). Excavations of the Vatican necropolis (photograph taken during the excavation). To the left of Peter's head is written PETRV, to the right, S ROGA; the rest of the epigraph was still covered with dirt.

often-visited churches there are convenient cards with an al-
ready-printed formula to which only the names of the persons need be added: "In the —— Church —— prayed for
——."

Scholars who have studied the ancient *tituli memoriales*
divide them into two classes, "Occidental and Oriental," according to whether they belong to the western or eastern
parts of the ancient world. Inscriptions of the first category
have the verb expressing memory in the indicative; those of
the second have it in the conjunctive and sometimes express
slightly different meanings. The Vatican graffito, with its
verb in the indicative, presents the classic formula of "Occidental" type and it is one of the very rare examples found
so far in Italy. Examples of the "occidental" style are abun-
dant in Greece and Egypt, but in Italy the only other ones
found—up to the present—are a pair from Pompeii and, perhaps, one at Naples.

A comparison with all the other known examples of the
"Occidental" formula shows with absolute certitude that the
place 'in the Vatican necropolis, where Lucius Paccius Eutychus wished to record his friend's name, was considered specially important. It was certainly a place where people went
to see something particularly beautiful, unusual or holy, a
place where prayers were offered and where distant friends
were remembered in prayer.

Was Lucius Paccius Eutychus a pagan or a Christian? If
he was a pagan, the inscription would have no meaning. This
section of the Vatican necropolis had no attraction for a
pagan; there was no famous shrine, no natural beauty, no
"curiosity" worth seeing. But if we consider the graffito
Christian, everything is easily explained; it is sufficient to
mention that Peter's Memorial is only a few steps away.

The Christian origin of the graffito is very clearly confirmed
by a detail of the same wall: the sketchy but unmistakable

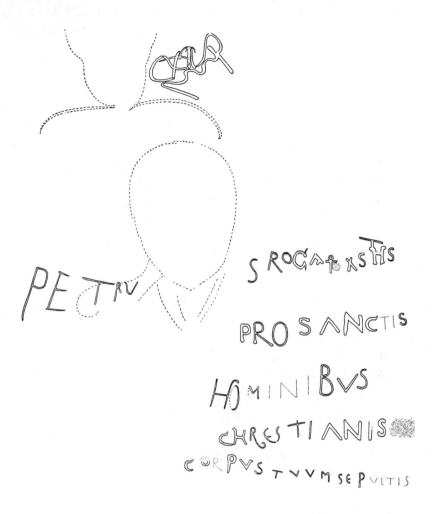

FIG. 44. Prayer to St. Peter in the tomb of the Valerii (end of the third, beginning of the fourth century A.D.). Excavations of the Vatican necropolis.

outline of a fish (Fig. 42), a symbol specially loved by the faithful who identified it with the Redeemer or with his followers, since each Christian is miraculously "fished" by the Divine Fisherman and reborn in the waters of Baptism.

The graffito of Lucius Paccius Eutychus is Christian, then, and it can only be interpreted in relation to the cult of St. Peter. It is important, therefore, to date it as precisely as possible.

Tomb R, on whose wall the graffito is carved, is earlier than the middle of the second century (about 130-150 A.D.), and the graffito seems to be almost equally old. Several elements testify to its antiquity: the epigraphic printing; the use of the Greek language which, as I have mentioned, is that of the earliest Christian inscriptions in Rome; the very name, Lucius Paccius Eutychus, which presents the so-called *tria nomina* (first name, family name and cognomen). It is known that in the names of freedmen, such as the writer of this graffito certainly was, the *tria nomina* tend to disappear at about the end of the second century.

Everything concurs, then, to lead us to the belief that the graffito on Tomb R was written during the second century. And from this fact a very attractive hypothesis rises spontaneously. I have already explained[20] that the Red Wall cut off access from the south to the open area, Field P, which is faced by the Apostolic Memorial. From that time on, the place sacred to Peter could not be reached directly by walking past Tomb R. It is reasonable to assume that our graffito was carved during the period when the faithful still passed that way to reach Field P. Therefore the graffito would be, like the wall on which it is carved, earlier than the construction of the Red Wall. Since the Red Wall can be dated certainly around 160, it is possible to place the graffito at least as far back as approximately 150 A.D.

So we can state that at that time, not more than eighty

FIG. 45. A mausoleum of the second burial place under the Church of St. Sebastian (second half of the second century A.D.).

years after the Apostle's death, pilgrims were already coming to the slopes of the Vatican Hill to do honor to the Martyr's Tomb. Eutychus was one of them: the first known to us of the countless pilgrims who have come, through the centuries, to visit the most sacred place in Rome.

D. *The Christian Evidence in the Tomb of the Valerii*

The tomb of the Valerii is one of the "mausolea" belonging to the necropolis discovered under the Vatican basilica. About twenty meters distant from the Apostolic Memorial, it can be dated between the reign of Marcus Aurelius (161-180 A.D.) and the beginning of the reign of Commodus (180-192 A.D.) It is certainly one of the richest and most beautiful structures in the entire necropolis. Its chief ornament is a series of magnificent plaster decorations (already mentioned when we were considering the necropolis in general).[21] For their artistic form and their representational content they are worthy of extended study.

The large marble plaque imbedded above the entrance informs us that this tomb belonged to *C. Valerius Herma* and his family.[22] Other inscriptions found about the edifice refer to members of this family or of related families. The first bodies to find a resting place within these walls were pagan, but as the new religion spread Christians were also buried there. I have already mentioned the sarcophagus of a certain *Valerinus Vasatulus* and the tombstone of a joyous Christian soul who, during his life, always joked and never quarreled.[23]

But the most noteworthy Christian evidence in the tomb of the Valerii is a series of inscriptions traced in red, done over in black. With the inscriptions there are two naïve portraits, one above the other; Christ above, St. Peter below (Fig. 43). The evidence which I mentioned is on the wall facing the entrance, in a niche which held the place of honor and in ancient times contained an elegant plaster figure of Apollo-Harpocrates. Most of the plaster has now fallen away, but the figure of this youthful god (a blending of the Greek Apollo with the Egyptian Harpocrates) can still be seen in outline. The pose is typical; he holds the index finger of his right hand up to his lips as though to silence visitors to this city of the dead, and in his left hand he has a bird.

Next to the right leg of this figure, on the left-hand side of the niche, is the Christian inscription. In the spring of 1952, when I saw it and, after reading, wished others to see it, the lines of red lead and black carbon were still quite visible. Ten years earlier, when first discovered, they must have been even fresher; but the decay commonly found in ancient pictures was accelerated in this case by the dampness of the place so that today the inscription has almost vanished.

Peter's head in the picture is that of an old bald man with a long beard. In the early Christian centuries the Apostle was generally depicted with a thick head of hair but there is also evidence of a tradition according to which he was bald. To the left of the head are the letters PETRV, and to the right

FIG. 46. Birds and fruit in a painting of the second burial place under the Church of St. Sebastian (second half of the second century A.D.).

the rest of the epigraph which is distributed through five lines (Fig. 44):

PETRVS ROGA ✝ XS IHS
PRO SANC(TI)S
HOM(INI)BVS
CHRESTIANIS AD
CO(R)PVS TVVM SEP (VLTIS)

"Peter pray for the pious Christian men buried near your body." At the end of the first line are abbreviated signs of Christ Jesus (XS IHS) accompanied by the sign of the *crux ansata,* an Egyptian symbol of salvation. The adjective *sanctis* is worthy of note; it does not mean the same as the modern word "saints," but rather all faithful members of the Church in general. Also worth mentioning is the form *Chrestianis,* rather than *Christianis.* But the most important fact is the existence in this place of a prayer to Peter as patron of the deceased, a prayer in which, besides, the nearness of the Martyr's tomb is mentioned.

The head of Peter is surmounted by a very unusual head of Christ. There are many things that could be said about this figure. Here it will be sufficient to recall that it bears the word VIBVS ("living") written on the forehead and is accompanied by the symbol of the Phoenix. This was a legendary bird which, according to the pagans, burned itself to rise again from its own ashes; a quality which led the Christians to adopt the Phoenix as a symbol of resurrection. We should not be surprised, then, to see the symbol of the Phoenix and the epithet VIBVS applied to Christ, considered as Life and Resurrection. We might also note that the proximity of Christ and Peter harmonizes fully with the graffiti on Wall G and other early Christian inscriptions which show us the Redeemer's name associated with that of His first vicar.

The very presence of this inscription in the tomb of the

FIG. 47. Graffiti on the walls of the *triclia* under the Church of St. Sebastian (second half of the third century A.D.). The graffito *Paule ed Petre petite pro Victore* ("Paul and Peter, pray for Victor") is quite visible.

Valerii informs us that a certain number of Christians were buried there. It is very probable that the presence of several Christian graves in this tomb led the survivors to direct this simple and trusting prayer to the Apostle. These graves might be identified with the many places for inhumation which, as I have already said,[24] were brought to light in the tomb of the Valerii by the most recent excavations. As for the age of the design on the wall, which seems to have been done at various times by various hands, not all at once by a single person, everything leads to the opinion that it can be dated, like the inscriptions on Wall G, between the end of the third and the beginning of the fourth century. In any case, it is previous to the covering over of the burial place and therefore confirms, once again, the fact that Peter was venerated in the Vatican even before Constantine had his great basilica built there.

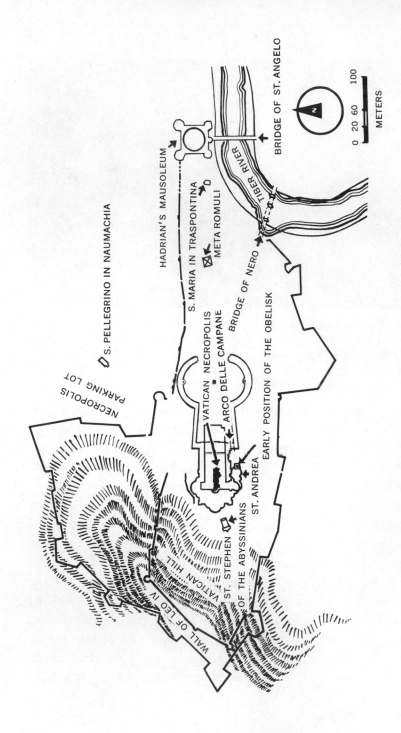

PLATE I. Map of the Vatican in Ancient Times.

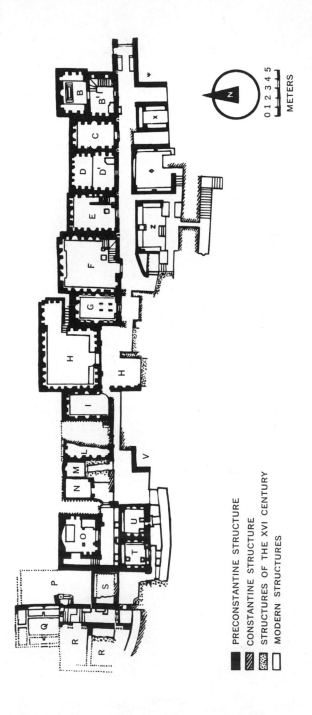

PLATE II. Diagram of the Cemetery under the Basilica.

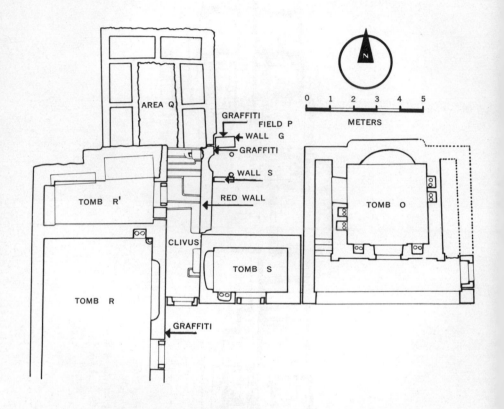

AREA Q

GRAFFITI
FIELD P
WALL G
GRAFFITI
WALL S
RED WALL

TOMB R'

TOMB R

CLIVUS

TOMB S

TOMB O

GRAFFITI

0 1 2 3 4 5

METERS

N

PLATE III. The Area of the Apostolic Memorial.

PLATE IV

PLATE V

PLATE VI

PLATE VII

PLATE VIII

PLATE IX

PLATE X

PLATE XI

PLATE XII

PLATE XIII

VI

THE CULT OF THE APOSTLES PETER
AND PAUL ON THE APPIAN WAY

A visitor to rome who goes out to the Appian Way to see
the remains of pagan and Christian antiquity usually visits
the Church of St. Sebastian, at the place usually called *in
Catacumbas*. He knows already, or he is soon told by the
guides that this church, built at the third mile of the Appian
Way, was once dedicated to the Apostles Peter and Paul, and
that it is one of the great Christian houses of prayer constructed by Constantine to express his gratitude for the victory at the Milvian Bridge (October 28, 312). Another bit of
information is usually added to this: that the remains of
Peter and Paul were kept there for a certain period—according to the most popular version, from 258 until the time of
Constantine. In 258, it is claimed, the remains were taken
from their respective tombs; and in the time of Constantine,
when the basilicas in the Vatican and on the Via Ostiense
were complete or nearing completion, they were brought
back to their original locations which had been made more
magnificent by the generous Emperor.

161

How much truth is there in all this?

That the basilica dedicated to Peter and Paul on the Appian way was built by Constantine is absolutely certain; but there is less certainty that the remains of the Apostles were actually kept there for a certain period. This question has been long and passionately discussed and it is not yet solved in all its details. Many scholars, some of them very reliable, have made rivers of ink flow, some confirming, some denying the story of the bodies' translation.

This is not the place to analyze the whole problem; it will be sufficient to clarify its principal elements and then to draw a conclusion wherever we can.

Let us examine first what we can find in ancient authors on the transfer of the bodies of the Apostles to the Appian Way.

The chief testimony is that of Pope Damasus. This great pontiff, who reigned from 366 to 384 and who, among other tasks, glorified the ancient martyrs in a series of epigrams written by himself, dedicated an epigram to the Apostles venerated on the Appian Way.[1] The original epigraphic text of the poem has been lost, but there is a partial copy at the church, preserved on a carved stone which can be dated in about the thirteenth century. Other copies have been handed down, with several variant readings, by certain ancient manuscripts. The most probable version of the epigram reads:

Hic habitare (or *habitasse*) *prius sanctos cognoscere debes*
nomina quisq(ue) Petri pariter Pauliq(ue) requiris.
Discipulos Oriens misit, quod sponte fatemur;
sanguinis ob meritum Xr(ist)um̄q(ue) per astra secuti
aetherios petiere sinus regnaque piorum:
Roma suos potius meruit defendere cives.
Haec Damasus vestras referat nova sidera laudes.[2]

Endless discussions have arisen about the word *habitare* (or *habitasse*). Some prefer the variant *habitare* (present infinitive) thinking that Damasus means "know that Peter and Paul dwell here (in a spiritual sense, i.e., are venerated here.)" Those who support the variant *habitasse* (perfect infinitive) may interpret this verb in a literal or figurative sense. According to some, Damasus is referring to a tradition that during their lives the Apostles lived at this site; according to others he is thinking of a mortuary dwelling, i.e., a tomb.

It must be admitted that Damasus' words are not a model of clarity. But one thing is very clear, that they make not the least mention of any transfer of the two holy bodies. And this is very significant. We must note that Damasus lived at a time when, without any hesitation or reservation, the faithful believed in the existence of the tombs of Peter and Paul respectively in the Vatican and on the Via Ostiense. For that reason he would certainly not have neglected to mention the transfer of the two holy relics if he truly had any information on it. His silence leads to the conclusion that he knew nothing about it.

After Damasus, other voices are raised from the fifth to seventh century to tell us of the Apostles in relation to the church on the Appian Way. But they are all voices that refer to the epigram of Damasus, either to clarify it or to embellish it with more or less colorful additions. It is interesting to note that even these late sources do not speak of a transfer of the holy remains in 258 A.D. If any hint can be found on the temporary entombment of Peter and Paul on the Appian Way, it is attributed to a time earlier than 258, sometimes immediately after the martyrdom of the Apostles; and in these cases the duration of their stay is kept to a minimum by those who tell of the transfer, to avoid dimming the glory universally attributed to the tombs in the Vatican and on the Via Ostiense.

In conclusion, the testimony of ancient authors is reduced (and only for those who prefer the variant *habitasse*) to the obscure hint from Damasus.

But how did the opinion arise that 258 was the year in which the remains of the Apostles were transferred to the Appian Way *in Catacumbas*?

The so-called Chronography of 354 is a collection of Roman religious feasts edited in 354 A.D. by Furius Dionysius Philocalus, the future secretary of Pope Damasus. Enumerating the feasts celebrated in honor of martyrs on the days on which each of them was placed in his tomb (*Depositio martyrum*), he has entered, for June 29, a feast of Peter in the Catacombs and of Paul on the Via Ostiense. Added to this note are the words *Tusco et Basso cons(ulibus)*,[3] which brings us to the year 258 A.D. in which Tuscus and Bassus were consuls. Although the Chronography was written in 354, it seems to reflect the situation in the years before 336. Another source, the so-called Martyrology of Jerome (a collection of martyrs' feasts which goes back, at most, to the beginning of the fifth century) records, on the date of June 29, a feast of Peter in the Vatican, one of Paul on the Via Ostiense, and a third of Peter and Paul at the Catacombs. It also adds a mention of the consuls Tuscus and Bassus, i.e., of the year 258 A.D.[4] While the Martyrology speaks of a common feast of Peter and Paul in the Catacombs, the Chronography mentions, as I have said, only a feast of Peter in the Catacombs and says nothing of the feast in the Vatican. Some scholars explain this silence ingeniously by asserting that in 354 (or 336?) the Vatican basilica was not yet finished and therefore the feast of Peter was still being celebrated, for the convenience of the faithful, in the church on the Appian Way. Be that as it may, there is still the puzzling date of 258. What significance can we attribute to it?

Evidently it marks the beginning of a common feast of

Peter and Paul in the region of the Catacombs. But a great student of Church history, Msgr. Louis Duchesne, sees something more in it. In his monumental edition of the *Liber Pontificalis,* whose first volume was printed in Paris in 1886, Duchesne[5] observes that in the years 257 and 258 the Christians suffered violent persecution under the emperor Valerian. In 257, he notes, an edict was issued forbidding the faithful to assemble in their cemeteries.[6] Since this was so, Duchesne observes, the Christians of Rome must have wanted to save the venerated remains of the Apostles from danger and may have taken them from the Vatican and the Via Ostiense to the Appian Way. The placing of the relics in the new tombs must have taken place on the date recorded in the Chronography and the Martyrology. Only in the time of Constantine, with the persecutions ended and peace established between the Empire and the Church (by the Edict of Milan in 313) would the precious remains have been brought back to their original resting places from the Appian Way.

Duchesne's conjecture had a very widespread response and occasioned a swarm of writings which has not yet ceased. Some scholars welcomed it enthusiastically, and even considered it a fact now beyond discussion; others rejected it as unsatisfactory or even absurd. And indeed the objections against this thesis cannot be ignored. First of all, the Chronography and the Martyrology tell us that June 29, the day on which the common martyrdom of the two Apostles is believed to have occurred, was celebrated as a feast in their honor in the Catacombs region, but they do not mention any transfer of their remains. And if this silence does not seem a very weighty point, it must also be mentioned that the hypothesis of transfer is, in itself, very improbable. In the first place, Valerian's edict forbade the Christians to hold meetings in their cemeteries, but it did not threaten their tombs; both Christian and pagan Romans had too great a respect for

tombs, too great a reluctance to trouble in any way the peace
of the dead. In the second place, it is hard to see what practical effect the transfer of the two bodies to the Catacombs
could have. Certainly they would not have been safer in the
Catacombs than they were in the Vatican and on the Via
Ostiense. Rather, since in both places the Apostle's tombs
were in the middle of pagan cemeteries, the faithful had the
advantage of being able to visit them freely without disobey-
ing the imperial edict. Besides, it is very difficult to believe
that the Christians would have exposed themselves, precisely
during a time of persecution, to the charge of disturbing
sepulchres. If they opened the tombs and transported their
contents from one end of Rome to the other, they would be
under the eyes of the imperial guards, who are known to
have had one of their stations at that time near the Catacombs, close to the still existing tomb of Cecilia Metella.

Another strong objection to the thesis of Duchesne and
his followers can be found in the very significant silence of
Eusebius, Bishop of Caesarea in Palestine. This learned historian of the Church preserved for us, as I have mentioned,[7]
a passage from Gaius, a churchman who lived in Rome at the
end of the second and beginning of the third century A.D.
This passage mentions the presence of Peter's and Paul's
tombs respectively in the Vatican and on the Via Ostiense.
Gaius' valuable words are included in a passage of the *Ecclesiastical History* of Eusebius, and in a part of it which is
dated between the years 310 and 312 A.D., approximately.
Now, Eusebius does not seem to know any other tradition on
the Apostle's tombs but that of Gaius: that is, he knows that
Peter's tomb is in the Vatican, Paul's on the Via Ostiense.
And this is quite important, since if the remains of the two
Apostles had really been on the Appian Way (according to
Duchesne's theory they would still be there in the period
310-312), Eusebius would certainly have known about it, and

would have passed on the information. In another work, the *Theophania,* written in 333, Eusebius speaks explicitly of the glorious tomb of Peter in the Vatican, remarking on the fervent devotion he received from all the faithful. I have quoted this passage at the beginning of this book.[8]

At the end of the fourth century, a hymn attributed to St. Ambrose tells us of a feast in honor of the Apostles celebrated simultaneously on "three roads," i.e., in the Vatican, on the Via Ostiense and on the Appian Way.[9] This information is substantially the same as that which we receive at the beginning of the next century from the Martyrology. At about the same time, the Christian poet Prudentius, in a hymn on the martyrdom of the two Apostles, refers to the feasts celebrated in their honor in the Vatican and on the Via Ostiense,[10] but he does not mention the feast on the Appian Way. This silence would seem to contrast with the data in the Martyrology and the Ambrosian hymn, but it may be explained by considering that the celebration of the feast on the Appian Way must by then have lost much of its importance compared to the feasts celebrated near the tombs of the Apostles in the Vatican and on the Via Ostiense.

As for the presumed return of the two bodies to their former resting places, it is not mentioned by any ancient author. This is not without meaning, since if these glorious remains had really been returned from the Appian Way to the two basilicas built in honor of the Apostles this return would have been an outstanding event and widely mentioned.

Now let us sum up the information we have from the authors:

1. There is no explicit record of a transfer, only a vague hint from Damasus (between the years 366 and 383) of the Apostles "dwelling" on the Appian Way;

2. There is definite mention of a feast in honor of the

two Apostles, instituted in 258 during the consulship of Tuscus and Bassus.

Now let us see what the excavations under the Church of
St. Sebastian add to the literary tradition.

Begun in 1892 and resumed after a long interruption in
1915, these excavations permit us to establish with sufficient
exactness what has happened in the area. In the first century
A.D., and perhaps even before, there was an ancient quarry
here, and it is quite probable that this excavation was the
origin of the Greek expression κατὰ κύμβας (kata kumbas—
"near the pit") which became the Latin in Catacumbas. After
a Christian cemetery was discovered in this part of the Appian Way, the name of "Catacomb" soon became synonymous
with Christian underground cemeteries in Rome and elsewhere.

During the first century A.D. and in the first half of the
second there were tombs in the vicinity of the pozzuolite
quarry, including some columbaria with their niches for cremation urns. At the same time there was another set of structures rising in the same area, being built with great care and
decorated with rather good pictures; the so-called Villa
Grande, whose purpose has not yet been very well explained.
Work on this unusual structure was suddenly interrupted
about the middle of the second century. The sections already
built and part of the neighboring cemetery were covered with
earth, and on the new level, between the end of the second
and the beginning of the third century, new tombs were
built. This time they were ornate mausolea (Fig. 45) decorated with plaster ornaments and pictures (Fig. 46) and
fairly similar to the tombs of the same period brought to
light by the recent excavations under St. Peter's Basilica.
Contemporary with these rich mausolea there are more mod-

est tombs and some installations certainly designed for holding funeral ceremonies.

All the tombs of the earlier burial place (previous to the
middle of the second century) are pagan. The first traces
of Christianity begin to appear only in the second burial
place, from the end of the second to the beginning of the
third century. But from the middle of the third century on,
after the second burial place was covered over, the new religion began to show itself with a fairly conspicuous set of
very interesting monuments. This group is unquestionably
the most important discovery of the excavations here.

On the level reached by the covering of the second cemetery, in a place that corresponds almost exactly to the center
of the present Church of St. Sebastian, the excavations have
brought to light a walled courtyard, roofless and paved with
bricks. Along the walls there are benches, protected by an
awning. Evidently associated with this structure were a well
and some remains that showed the existence of a kitchen at
one time. Evidently, this was a place used for simple banquets, one of the places called *tricliae* by the Romans. The
walls of this *triclia* were painted, and on the painting many
graffiti had been carved in the course of time. These graffiti
contain invocations by the faithful to the Apostles Peter and
Paul for the salvation of living and dead persons: "Paul and
Peter, pray for Victor," "Peter and Paul, remember Antonius
Bassus," etc. Along with the requests for prayers were records of *refrigeria* held in this place: for example, "To Peter
and Paul I, Tomius Celius, made a *refrigerium*," "Near Paul
and Peter I made a *refrigerium*," and so forth (Fig. 47).

In the vocabulary of the ancient Christians, *refrigerium*
usually signifies the reward and comforts of heaven, the
eternal "coolness" invoked by the faithful for the dead. But
here we are dealing with something else. The term *refrig-*

erium seems to have a specialized meaning, indicating a
funeral banquet. This interpretation is confirmed by the
presence of the *triclia*. The very ancient practice of holding
funeral banquets was widespread among the pagans and
lasted well into the Christian era although it was rather seriously opposed by the Church. As for the *refrigeria* of St.
Sebastian's, naturally they were not intended to help the
Apostles, who had no need of help; but rather to honor them,
with the probable purpose of thus aiding the souls of the deceased. It is quite possible, indeed even very probable that
the joy of the banquet sometimes went beyond the limits required by respect for a holy place. At a later date, in Carthage,
St. Augustine had to complain of the wild bonfires set on the
feasts of martyrs and of noisy banquets held right inside the
churches. Something of this sort may have taken place here.

The spiritual center of the joyful celebrations in honor
of SS. Peter and Paul on the Appian Way seems to have been
a monument facing south near the entrance to the *triclia;*
a sort of little shrine flanked by two small blind arches covered with marble and mosaics on the inside. Some scholars
have described this monument as a *mensa martyrum,* but in
reality it is hard to state its exact nature. We can only be
fairly certain that the two arches served to guard something
connected with each of the Apostles. The richness of the
marble and mosaics with which they are decorated testifies
to this. There is a sharp contrast between this richness and
the simplicity, I might almost say the poverty, of the rest of
the structure.

Those who support the theory that the Apostles' bodies
were kept for some time in this region of the Appian Way
conducted a long search for the two special tombs throughout
the vast area of St. Sebastian's. But their researches have remained completely unsuccessful, and this negative result has

strengthened the opinion that the true center of the cult must have been the monument with the two little arches.

To establish the level on which the *triclia* was built, it was necessary, as I have said, to fill in the second-stage burial place with dirt, covering the rich mausolea and the more modest tombs. Built about the middle of the third century, the *triclia* was used through that century and into the first years of the fourth. At the time of Constantine, from about 315 to 325 A.D., it was buried, in its turn, to form the level on which the basilica in honor of Peter and Paul was built. The Christian cult based on the practice of *refrigerium* had lasted, therefore, only a few decades.

The basilica erected by Constantine in honor of the Apostles soon became a burial place and its exterior was circled with a crown of mausolea. Much later, in the ninth century, the modern name of St. Sebastian was substituted for those of Peter and Paul, in honor of the famous martyr, killed during the persecutions of Diocletian, who had been buried at that part of the Appian Way and who soon attracted the veneration of the faithful to his glorious tomb.

That, in summary, is what can be deduced from the archaeological investigations carried out under the Basilica of St. Sebastian.

Clearly, these results are totally negative on the question of whether the Apostles' bodies were ever transferred. In this, they agree perfectly with the data of the literary sources. In other words, the authors and the excavations offer no explicit evidence that the remains of Peter and Paul were transported, during the third century to this part of the Appian Way and later returned, during the age of Constantine, to their original resting places.

In addition, as far as St. Peter is concerned, it can be demonstrated that from the second century onward the faithful in Rome have believed without question that his remains were in the Vatican; naturally this weakens the transfer theory. Besides the famous passage from Gaius, which I have already mentioned,[11] this belief is shown by many pieces of evidence uncovered during the excavations under St. Peter's Basilica. Let us look at the evidence in chronological order:

a. The graffito on the Red Wall (about 160 A.D.);
b. The passage from Gaius (about 200 A.D.);
c. The rich Christian decoration in the tomb of the Julii (first half of the third century);
d. The graffiti on Wall G and the Christian inscription in the tomb of the Valerii (end of the third, beginning of the fourth century).

All these sources indicate the common belief that Peter's remains were in the Vatican. In addition, the graffiti carved on an outside wall of Tomb R demonstrate, as we have seen, the existence of a Christian cult, evidently connected with the Apostle's tomb, in about 150 A.D. and perhaps even earlier.[12]

In this closely-linked chain of evidence testifying to Peter's presence in the Vatican it would be difficult to insert the (poorly attested) episode of a transfer. In addition, the graffiti on Wall G and the Christian evidence in the tomb of the Valerii, approximately contemporary with the graffiti on the Appian Way, speak of the burial of Peter in the Vatican as they certainly would not if the faithful of that time had known the Apostle's remains to be in the sanctuary in Catacumbas. Finally, it must be considered that the graffiti in the Vatican are on a much higher spiritual level than those on the Appian Way. This deeper spirituality also favors the theory that the faithful considered the Vatican the only place where Peter had been entombed.

Then what is the devotion to Peter and Paul that began in 258 on the Appian Way?

FIG. 48. The Apostles Peter (right) and Paul, in a medallion found in the cemetery of Domitilla (beginning of the third century A.D.). Sacred Museum of the Vatican Library.

Above all, it must be borne in mind that it is a joint devotion to both Apostles. We have seen that even in the earliest times St. Clement of Rome and St. Ignatius of Antioch, as well as Gaius, did not hesitate to unite Peter and Paul in a single memory;[13] but 258 may have marked the beginning of a true and proper devotion to the two Martyrs whom the Church considered its brightest luminaries. And indeed it can be established, from other evidence, that the cult of the martyrs, although it was practiced in Rome from the most ancient times, acquired a greater development and a more clearly defined character precisely during the first half of the third century.

In addition, the existence of a burial place for the Popes

in the nearby cemetery of St. Callistus certainly contributed to the origin of the devotion to Peter and Paul on the Appian Way. Already in 217, when Pope St. Zephyrinus died, his body had been placed in this cemetery on the Appian Way; but the idea of building a special crypt there did not occur until some years later, and the first Pope buried in this crypt was Anteros who died in 236. The year 258, in which the joint cult of Peter and Paul was instituted is also a memorable date for the crypt of the Popes: the martyr Sixtus II was laid to rest there in that year. The persecution of Valerian was raging at the time, and Sixtus II, defying the imperial edict which forbade Christians to hold meetings in their own cemeteries,[14] had gone with some deacons to the cemetery of St. Callistus to officiate near the tombs of his predecessors. There he had been captured and barbarously killed with his companions a short time thereafter, on August 6, 258.[15] The coincidence of the two events may not be merely casual. It is probable that the heroic death of Sixtus II aroused in the

FIG. 49. The Apostles Peter and Paul on either side of a wreath bearing the monogram of Christ. Gilded glass, from the fourth century A.D.

FIG. 50. Tombstone of Pope Anteros (died 236 A.D.). Rome, cemetery of St. Callistus, crypt of the Popes. After the Greek name Ἀντέρως (Anteros) are written the first three letters of the word ἐπίσκοπος (*episkopos* = "bishop"). This was the title given to the early Popes.

faithful a desire to establish a devotion to the two Chiefs of the Apostles near the place where, since 217 A.D., the Popes were being buried, where, that very year, a new, glorious martyr had been laid to rest.

Since the edict of Valerian forbade Christians to meet in their cemeteries, the new devotion obviously could not be started in the Cemetery of St. Callistus. For reasons unknown to us, the choice fell to the nearby location *in Catacumbas*. The tombs were covered over and on the new level, thus formed, the devotion to the Apostles was organized. Those who hold the thesis that the remains of Peter and Paul were totally or partially transferred to this place in 258 stress the very serious decision taken at that time to cover the former burial place. Only an exceptional motive, such as the transfer of the Apostles' remains, could have lead to such an action, they claim. But this type of explanation does not seem necessary, particularly since, at an earlier date, in the second century, a similar event had taken place: the covering of earlier tombs and the interruption of work on the so-called Villa Grande to create a new level for the building of the rich mausolea of the second burial place. Naturally we must recognize that, by the middle of the third century, the Christians must have been the proprietors of the region *in Catacumbas*; otherwise they would not have been able to sacrifice an entire cemetery even for the noble and heartfelt purpose of establishing devotion to the Apostles in that area.

Although the cemetery was completely buried, the new cult still had a funereal character. In the first place, its high point was on June 29, the day on which, according to tradition, the two Apostles suffered martyrdom. In addition, the most characteristic rite of the feast was that of a funeral banquet: the *refrigerium*. Finally, the evident relation of the Apostles' shrine to the neighboring Crypt of the Popes confirms the funereal character of the cult itself.

But all this does not force us to believe that the bodies of the Apostles had been transferred to the Appian Way, and it can easily be maintained that the devotion centered (as sometimes occurred) on a cenotaph, or, at most, on a few relics. In the latter case, it might be well to think of objects (such as medals, pieces of cloth, etc.) which had been in contact with the true tombs of Peter and Paul, probably not of relics actually taken from their tombs. The unauthorized opening of tombs would have been too difficult and too dangerous in that time of persecution. The fact that the feast of June 29 on the Appian Way is recorded in the *Chronography of 354* together with those which were celebrated at the actual tombs of the martyrs does not prove the presence of the holy remains in the shrine *in Catacumbas,* since this same Chronog-

raphy also records the feasts of three martyrs—Cyprian, Felic-
itas and Perpetua—whose tombs were generally known to
be in Africa, very far from Rome. It would also be an error
to give decisive importance to the expression "near to Peter
and Paul," which occurs, as we have seen, in a graffito of the
triclia. It does not necessarily mean "near the tombs of Peter
and Paul," but could rather indicate only the place where
devotion to the Apostles flourished, perhaps with the aid of
some "relics." This interpretation is well supported by an
ancient Christian sepulchral inscription in Algeria which
speaks of a child buried by his parents "near Saints Peter and
Paul."[16] In this case, naturally we cannot find a reference to
the true tombs of the Apostles; the expression must have been
suggested by the presence of some sort of "relics" of the two
outstanding martyrs—an explanation which can have equal
validity for the graffito in the *triclia*. Finally, the monument
with the two little arches which was found near the *triclia*
and which seems to have been the center of the devotion to
Peter and Paul hardly justifies the concept of two true tombs,
while on the other hand it could very appropriately be considered a repository for "relics."

Summing up all that is known on the devotion to the
Apostles *in Catacumbas,* we can establish the following:

In 258, during the consulate of Tuscus and Bassus, a devotion to Peter and Paul was instituted. June 29, the date given
for the double martyrdom of the Apostles, was chosen as the
date for the feast. The devotion was established at the third
mile of the Appian Way, in the place called *in Catacumbas.*
The reasons for choosing this site are no longer very clear.
We can only assume that the nearness of the Cemetery of St.
Callistus had something to do with the choice. Since the year
217, it had been customary to bury deceased pontiffs in this
cemetery, and there was a Papal Crypt in which, precisely in

the year 258, the martyr Sixtus II had been laid to rest. Certainly the devotion to the two greatest luminaries of the Church would have been better situated right in the Cemetery of Callistus; but, since the very recent edict of Valerian forbade the Christians to meet in their own cemeteries, a nearby location had to be chosen. This was the area *in Catacumbas.* There was also a cemetery here, but the Christians, who must have owned it, covered it over and built a shrine to the Apostles on the new level. The new devotion had a funereal aspect, characterized by the practice of the *refrigerium.* This aspect can be explained without recourse to the thesis (very improbable and certainly not proved) of a transfer of the Apostles' bodies from their original locations. It is sufficient to reflect that the new feast was established to commemorate the glorious deaths of Peter and Paul, and that undoubtedly it had some connection with the tombs of the Popes in the nearby Cemetery of St. Callistus. The material center of the devotion must have been various "relics" of the Apostles kept in a typical monument with two small arches. The devotion itself did not last very long: from 258 to about 320 A.D. At the latter date, the *triclia* was buried to make room for Constantine's basilica in honor of Peter and Paul. In the ninth century, this basilica was given the name of St. Sebastian, in homage of the martyr who had been buried there during the persecution of Diocletian at the beginning of the fourth century, and whose tomb had attracted those of many other Christians.

Although there is not sufficient evidence to prove that the remains of Peter and Paul were kept for some time *in Catacumbas* on the site of the present Church of St. Sebastian, this region of the Appian Way can still claim the glory of having first given impetus to the devotion which associates Peter and Paul in the glory of martyrdom and in the supreme dignity of Princes of the Apostles.

VII

~

CONCLUSIONS

IN WRITING THESE PAGES, I have attempted to bring out a few points of particular importance. Now I would like to summarize them, to permit the reader more easily to evaluate the complex problem of the final events in the life of the Apostle Peter and the beginnings of the devotion he has received and continues to receive from the faithful.

There are many authoritative writers who testify to the fact that Peter came to Rome to bring the message of Christ, and that he suffered martyrdom in Rome during the reign of Nero (54-68). By comparing the testimony of St. Clement of Rome (about 96 A.D.) with a passage in the *Annals* of Tacitus, it can be established that the Apostle's martyrdom took place in the Vatican, more exactly, in the famous Gardens of Nero (perhaps in the arena which was its chief attraction), during one of those cruel exhibitions which—following the burning of Rome (July, 64 A.D.)—the Emperor had arranged to appease the angry populace. From the testimony of various authors it can also be established with certitude that Peter was crucified.

Peter's crucifixion is an important point in considering the question of his burial. One of the major arguments against the existence of the Apostle's tomb is that there can be no tomb of Peter simply because it would have been physically impossible to recognize the Martyr's body in the pile of human flesh at the end of the spectacle. This argument has little force because the martyrs must have been accompanied until the very end by the pitying care of the faithful. And in the case of Peter the argument is even less effective because the body of a man hung on a cross could easily be recovered and buried.

The site of Peter's burial was in the Vatican. The most ancient author who gives us this information is Gaius, a churchman of Rome who lived during the time of Pope Zephyrinus (198-217); and the fact is confirmed by excavations under the basilica, which offer the following evidence:

1. A burial place whose most ancient tombs date back to the first century (i.e., the century in which the Apostle died). This burial place is under the basilica and in its immediate vicinity.

2. A memorial shrine erected about 160 A.D., which can be certainly identified with the "trophy" of Gaius, is situated directly under the papal altar in the present basilica.

3. Under the shrine there are traces of an ancient grave; this grave seems to have been an object of very special respect.

4. A Greek inscription, carved on a wall next to the chapel and datable about 160 A.D., states that "Peter is within."

5. A wall (the so-called Wall G) very near to the shrine, is literally crowded with Christian inscriptions, written in a very simple and meaningful cryptography, used by the faithful to express their deepest religious feelings. (The cryptography in these inscriptions has given us the key to interpret other cryptographic inscriptions in Rome and elsewhere.) The inscriptions on Wall G, datable between the end of the third and the beginning of the fourth century, contain a

precious historical reference in the famous expression *hoc vince,* referring to the vision of Constantine (October, 312). As for Peter, the principal themes recurring on the wall are: the intimate union of Peter and Christ; the keys of Peter; the victory of Christ, Peter and Mary; the life of souls in Christ and in Peter. There is also a mention of the Apostle's tomb on Wall G.

6. A large number of coins, datable from the first to the fifteenth century, were found near the shrine, where they were certainly left by countless pilgrims who came, through the centuries, to venerate the place sacred to the Apostle.

7. A Greek inscription, datable about 150 A.D. and carved on the outside wall of a tomb very close to the shrine, shows that this site was then a destination of Christian pilgrimages.

8. A small but richly decorated tomb (that of the Julii) was crowded in a totally irrational way between two previously existing tombs near the shrine. The expense lavished on this tiny building, and its awkward position, are clearly justified by the exceptional importance Christians attributed to this place.

9. A group of Christian inscriptions, which can be dated at the end of the third and beginning of the fourth century, is found in one of the tombs (that of the Valerii) in the necropolis under the basilica. One of these inscriptions, accompanied by a naïve drawing of Peter, contains a prayer to the Apostle for Christians buried near his body. Christ is associated with Peter, the head of the Redeemer being drawn above that of the Apostle, with the sign of the Phoenix, the mythical bird symbolizing resurrection.

From all these elements it becomes clear that, at least since the middle of the second century, the faithful have been convinced that St. Peter's tomb was in the Vatican necropolis; more precisely, at the place marked by the chapel under the present papal altar. When we go back to the faithful of the second century, this belief becomes very important, considering that they were extremely close to the date of Peter's martyrdom (65 or 67 A.D.) and must have been well-informed —from stories told by their fathers, if from no other source— on the circumstances of the Apostle's death. The intensity of their devotion to the Martyr is shown clearly (at least for the period around the end of the third and beginning of the fourth century) by the graffiti on Wall G. In these inscriptions, the faithful poured forth the fullness of their religious feelings, apparently wishing to proclaim their faith near the tomb of Christ's Vicar.

These graffiti, and also the Christian evidence in the tomb of the Valerii, make it obvious that at the end of the third and beginning of the fourth century, Christians recognized and honored the Martyr's tomb in the Vatican. According to a widespread modern opinion, the Apostle's remains were kept—at precisely this time—on the Appian Way, where the Church of St. Sebastian now stands. Peter's body, with that of Paul, is supposed to have been placed there in the year 258, during the persecution of the Emperor Valerian. Against this theory, which literary sources and the results of excavations have already shown to be poorly-founded, we now have the added testimony of the Vatican inscriptions. All that can be said with certitude is that, in 258 a combined devotion to the two Apostles was begun on the Appian Way, probably centering on various "relics."

The faithful who come to the Vatican basilica today consider the altar of the Confession a monument marking the most sacred spot in the immense building. This altar, protected by Bernini's ornate baldacchino and crowned by Michelangelo's dome, was built by Clement VIII (1592-1605). It is the lastest in a series of monuments, placed one above the other. In descending order, i.e., going backward through the centuries, we can establish this sequence:

A. The altar of Clement VIII (1592-1605) which stands in the present basilica;

B. The altar of Callistus II (1119-1124);

C. The altar of St. Gregory the Great (590-604);

D. The monument erected by the Emperor Constantine in honor of the Apostle (about 315 A.D.);

E. The shrine, which can be identified with the "trophy" of Peter mentioned by Gaius (about 160 A.D.);

F. A grave dug during the first century.

Over a humble first century grave, therefore, we find an uninterrupted series of monuments which rise, step by step, to the level of our own time: eloquent witnesses of a certitude which has been kept intact, down through the generations, to the present.

At the beginning of these pages, I asked whether or not we can accept the tradition that St. Peter's tomb is at the heart of the Vatican basilica. I stated that only a very careful study of the evidence could give us an exhaustive answer.

At the end of that study, I can state that the tradition is acceptable; indeed, that an objective examination of the evidence has greatly increased its strength and its value. Prescinding from a few points which have not yet been completely clarified (let us hope that they will be, by further excavations and new discoveries) we can now say that in the investigation of St. Peter's tomb Science has come to the aid of Faith. This happy alliance has placed on age-old tradition a strengthened and renewed seal of irrefutable Truth.

NOTES

Notes to the Preface

1. EUSEBIUS, *Theophania*, IV, 7 (ed. by E. Klostermann, in *Die griechischen christlichen Schriftsteller der ersten drei Jahrhunderte. Eusebius III,* Leipzig 1904, pp. 175*, 3-7).
2. LUTHER: *Against the Roman Papacy Instituted by the Devil,* Wittenberg 1545 (in E. MÜLHAUPT, *Luthers Evangelien-Auslegung,* II (1947) page 551).
3. K. HEUSSI, *Die römische Petrustradition in kritischer Sicht,* Tübingen 1955.
4. J. LIETZMANN, *Petrus römischer Märtyrer,* in *Sitzungsberichte der Berliner Akademie,* 1936, n. XXIX.
5. K. ALAND, *Petrus in Rom,* in *Historische Zeitschrift,* CLXXIII (1957) pp. 497-516.

Notes to I, The Testimony of Ancient Authors

1. ST. PAUL, Epistle to the Romans, XV 20.
2. ST. PETER, First Epistle, V 13.
3. So we are informed by FLAVIUS JOSEPHUS, *Jewish Antiquities,* XVIII 9, 8.
4. STRABO, *Geography,* XVII 807, 812; etc.
5. A book by H. FUCHS, *Der geistige Widerstand gegen Rom in der antiken Welt,* Berlin, 1938, is devoted to this interesting subject.
6. ST. JOHN, Gospel, XXI, 18 ff.
7. SAINT PETER, Second Epistle, I 14.
8. ST. CLEMENT, First Epistle to the Corinthians, 5 ff. (in *Patrologia graeca,* I, columns 217 A-221 A).
9. TACITUS, *Annals,* XV 44.
10. ST. PAUL, Second Epistle to the Corinthians, XI 26.

11. ST. PAUL, Epistle to the Philippians, I 15-17.
12. ST. IGNATIUS, *Epistle to the Romans*, 4 (in *Patrologia graeca*, V, col. 689 A-B).
13. E. PETERSON, *Das Martyrium des hl. Petrus nach der Petrus-Apocalypse* (in *Miscellanea G. Belvederi*, Rome 1954, pp. 181-185).
14. *Ascension of Isaias*, IV 2 ff. (ed. by E. TISSERANT, *Ascension d'Isaie*, Paris, 1909, pp. 116 ff.).
15. This passage from the *Apocalypse of Peter* is found in a papyrus of the Rainer Collection (C. WESSELY, in *Patrologia orientalis*, XVIII 3, Paris 1924, pp. 482 ff.)
16. The passage from the Bishop Dionysus comes down to us through EUSEBIUS, Bishop of Caesarea in Palestine, in his *Ecclesiastical History*, II 25, 8 (in *Patrologia graeca*, XX 209 A).
17. ST. IRENAEUS, *Against Heresies*, III 1-3 (in *Patrologia graeca*, VII, col. 844 A-855 A).
18. TERTULLIAN, *Concerning Prescriptions Against Heretics*, 36 (in *Patrologia latina*, II, col. 58 B-59 A); *Against the Gnostics (Scorpiace)*, 15 (op. cit., II, col. 174 B-175 B); *Against Marcion*, IV 5 (op. cit., II, col. 395 C).
19. L. VOUAUX, *Les Actes de Pierre*, Paris 1922, pp. 458-460.
20. ST. JOHN, *Apocalypse*, XI 3-13.
21. See note 6.
22. The information comes to us, indirectly, through MACARIUS of Magnesia, *Apocriticus*, III 22. This work reflects the attitudes of Porphyry.
23. TACITUS, *Annals*, XV 44.
24. This information has been transmitted to us by EUSEBIUS in his *Ecclesiastical History*, III 1, 2 (in *Patrologia graeca*, XX 216 A).
25. The Colosseum did not exist in the time of Nero.
26. PSEUDO-LINUS, *Saint Peter's Martyrdom*, 10 (in R. A. LIPSIUS, *Acta Petri* etc., Leipzig 1891, pp. 11 ff.)
27. ST. JEROME, *On Illustrious Men*, 1 (in *Patrologia latina*, XXIII, col. 639 A).
28. *Liber pontificalis*, Peter, VI (ed. by L. DUCHESNE, I, Paris 1955, p. 118).
29. JULIAN THE APOSTATE, *Against the Galileans*, 327 B.
30. TERTULLIAN, *On Modesty*, 21 (in *Patrologia latina*, II, col. 1078 C-1079 A).
31. EUSEBIUS, *Ecclesiastical History*, II 25, 5-7 (in *Patrologia graeca*, XX, col. 208-209).
32. See pp. 131-6.
33. PSEUDO-MARCELLUS, *Passion of the Holy Apostles Peter and Paul*, 63 (in R.A. LIPSIUS, op. cit., p. 173).
34. See p. 50.
35. See figures on pp. 53 and 56.
36. See p. 38.
37. See p. 58.

NOTES TO II, THE VATICAN IN ANCIENT TIMES

1. PLINY THE ELDER, *Natural History,* XVI 237.
2. TACITUS, *Histories,* II, 93, 2.
3. PLINY THE ELDER, op. cit., VIII 37.
4. MARTIAL, *Epigrams,* X 45, 5; VI 92, 3.
5. JUVENAL, *Satires,* VI 344.
6. PLINY THE YOUNGER, *Epistles,* IV 2, 5.
7. TACITUS, *Annals,* XIV 14.
8. See pp. 30, 36, 37.
9. PLINY THE ELDER, *Natural History,* XVI 201.
10. *Corpus Inscriptionum Latinarum,* VI 882.
11. DIO CASSIUS, *Roman History,* LIX 14.
12. ELIUS LAMPRIDIUS, *Life of Heliogabalus,* XXIII 1.
13. Not one but two *Naumachiae* are mentioned in the *Catalogue of the Fourteen Regions of Rome* (a catalogue of noteworthy things in the City, apparently compiled at the beginning of the fourth century) as located in the fourteenth region, which included the Vatican and the rest of the area on that side of the Tiber. The problem of this twofold *Naumachia* has not yet been solved (cf. R. VALENTINI and G. ZUCCHETTI, *Codice topografico della Città di Roma,* I, Rome 1940, pp. 144, 182.)
14. *Corpus Inscriptionum Latinarum,* XIII 1751.
15. *Corpus Inscriptionum Latinarum,* VI 497-504. Other inscriptions of this series, discovered in 1949, are mentioned in *Esplorazioni sotto la Confessione di san Pietro in Vaticano,* Vatican City 1951, Vol. I, pp. 14 ff., figures 2, 3.
16. I have dealt with this problem at some length in my monograph *Cristo e san Pietro in un documento precostantiniano della necropoli vaticana,* Rome 1953, pp. 65-69.
17. See p. 43.
18. The researches referred to are discussed in my article *Documenti del I secolo nella necropoli vaticana,* in *Rendiconti della Pontificia Accademia romana di archeologia,* Vol. XXIX (1956-1957), pp. 111-137.
19. *Corpus Inscriptionum Latinarum,* XV 1, n. 1273 a.

NOTES TO III, THE NECROPOLIS UNDER THE BASILICA

1. *Corpus Inscriptionum Latinorum,* VI 17985 a.
2. See p. 45.
3. See pp. 54, 55-9.
4. See pp. 49 ff.
5. See pp. 145-7.
6. See pp. 60 ff.

NOTES TO IV, THE APOSTLE'S MEMORIAL

1. *Corpus Inscriptionum Latinarum,* XV 1, n. 401.
2. See p. 62.

3. See above, pp. 136-44. The term "graffito" will appear frequently in the following pages, and perhaps a word of explanation is in order here. The Italian word is used in the translation because no exact English equivalent exists and because the term "graffito" is commonly used by English-speaking scholars. Based on an Italian word meaning "scratch," this word designates a class of inscriptions found on walls and similar surfaces; usually carved or scratched into the surface, sometimes written upon it. A graffito may include pictures or other symbols as well as words. It differs from other inscriptions usually by being more ephemeral, less formal, the work of amateurs moved by a passing fancy. A well-known modern graffito that may provide headaches for archaeologists of a future generation is the inscription: *Kilroy was here.* (Translator's note.)

4. *Corpus Inscriptionum Latinarum,* XV 1, n. 1120 a.

5. See pp. 55-8.

6. See pp. 56-9.

7. See pp. 39-41.

8. *Liber Pontificalis,* Anacletus (ed. by L. DUCHESNE, 1², Paris 1955, p. 125).

9. Cf. J. TOYNBEE and J. B. WARD PERKINS, *The Shrine of St. Peter and the Vatican Excavations,* London—New York—Toronto 1956, p. 157.

10. See pp. 39 ff., 88-9.

11. See pp. 131-6.

12. See pp. 31 ff.

13. See pp. 55-9, 84 ff.

Notes to V, The Testimony of the Inscriptions

1. See p. 90.

2. See pp. 79, 86.

3. See p. 90.

4. See p. 79.

5. See pp. 161, 165, 168.

6. PSEUDO-BARNABAS, *Epistle,* IX 8 (in *Patrologia Graeca,* II, col. 752 A-B).

7. ST. MATTHEW, *Gospel,* XVI 19.

8. See p. 79.

9. EUSEBIUS, *Life of Constantine,* I 28 (in *Patrologia Graeca,* XX, col. 944 B-C).

10. LACTANTIUS, *On the Deaths of Persecutors,* XLIV 4, ff. (in *Patrologia Latina,* VII, col. 260 B-261 A.)

11. *Corpus Inscriptionum Latinarum,* VI 1139.

12. NAZARIUS, *Panegyric,* XIII 2.

13. PRUDENTIUS, *Against Symmachus,* I 467 and 495 (in *Patrologia Latina,* LX 157 A, 159 A.)

14. See pp. 168, 171 ff., and Fig. 47.

15. See pp. 122 ff.

16. See pp. 95-6.

17. See p. 80.

18. See p. 39.
19. See p. 80 ff.
20. See p. 81.
21. See p. 69.
22. See p. 69 (Fig. 16.)
23. See p. 73.
24. See p. 71.

NOTES TO VI, THE CULT OF THE APOSTLES PETER AND PAUL ON THE APPIAN WAY

1. ST. DAMASUS, *Poems*, 9 (in *Patrologia Latina*, XIII, cols. 382 A-383 A). Cf. the edition by A. FERRUA, Vatican City 1942, pp. 139-144, n. 20.

2. The following is a tentative translation: "You, whoever you may be, who seek the names of Peter and Paul together, must know first of all that they dwell (or, accepting the variation *habitasse:* "formerly dwelt") here. The Orient sent them as disciples (i.e., of Christ): we admit it willingly. But, shedding their blood and following Christ through the stars, they have reached the bosom of heaven and the kingdom of the blessed. Rome has deserved to claim them as her citizens. Damasus thus speaks your praises, O new stars."

3. *Chronography of 354*, under the date June 29 (from TH. MOMMSEN, in *Monumenta Germaniae Historica*, Auctores Antiquissimi, IX 1, p. 71).

4. *Martyrology of Jerome* (in *Acta Sanctorum*, November II 2.)

5. L. DUCHESNE, *Liber Pontificalis*, I, Paris 1886 (second edition, 1955), pp. CIV-CVII.

6. EUSEBIUS, *Ecclesiastical History*, VII 11, 4 (in *Patrologia Graeca*, XX, col. 666 B-C); *Acts of St. Cyprian*, 1 (ed. by G. HARTEL, Vienna 1871, p. CXI).

7. See pp. 39-40.

8. See p. 5.

9. ST. AMBROSE (?), *Hymns*, 71 (in *Patrologia Latina*, XVII, col. 1253 ff.).

10. PRUDENTIUS, *Peristephanon*, hymn 12 (in *Patrologia Latina*, LX, col. 556 A-569 A).

11. See p. 39.

12. See pp. 142-4.

13. See pp. 29-33, 39.

14. See p. 165.

15. *Liber Pontificalis*, Sixtus II, II (ed. by L. DUCHESNE, I², Paris 1955, p. 155).

16. *Corpus Inscriptionum Latinarum*, VIII 9715, and supplement on page 2034. Cf. W. H. FREND, *The 'Memoriae Apostolorum' in Roman North Africa*, in "Journal of Roman Studies," XXX (1940), pp. 32-49.

BIBLIOGRAPHY

Much has been written on various topics treated in this book. The volumes here cited are grouped according to the various chapters to which they refer and are arranged in chronological order. The criterion of choice has been to include mainly books which have either introduced new elements into the study of the subject or clearly summarized what is already known.

I. The Testimony of Ancient Authors

H. LIETZMANN, *Petrus und Paulus in Rom,* second edition, Berlin-Leipzig 1927, pp. 226-237.
———— *Petrus römischer Märtyrer,* in "Sitzungsberichte der Preussischen Akademie der Wissenschaften," 1936, XXIX, pp. 392-410.
O. CULLMANN, *Petrus: Jünger-Apostel-Märtyrer,* Zurich 1952, pp. 73-135.
K. ALAND, *Petrus in Rom,* in "Historische Zeitschrift," CLXXXIII (1957), pp. 497-516.
A. RIMOLDI, *L'Apostolo san Pietro,* in "Analecta Gregoriana," vol. XCVI, Rome 1958.

II. The Vatican in Antiquity

G. LUGLI, *Il Vaticano nell'antichità classica,* in the volume *Vaticano* (prepared by G. FALLANI and M. ESCOBAR, Florence 1946, pp. 3-22).
E. JOSI, in *Enciclopedia cattolica,* under *Vaticano,* columns 1053-1060 (1954).

G. RADKE, in Pauly-Wissowa, *Realencyclopädie der classischen Altertumswissenschaft,* under *Vaticanus* 1, columns 490-493 (1955).

M. GUARDUCCI, *Documenti del I secolo nella necropoli vaticana,* in "Rendiconti della Pontificia Accademia romana di archeologia," vol. XXIX (1956-57), pp. 111-137.

F. MAGI, *Relazione preliminare sui ritrovamenti archeologici nell'area dell'autoparco vaticano,* in *Triplice omaggio a Sua Santità Pio XII,* Vatican City 1958, Vol. II, pp. 87-99 (with 14 plates).

III. THE NECROPOLIS UNDER THE BASILICA

IV. THE APOSTLE'S MEMORIAL

B.M. APPOLLONJ GHETTI, A. FERRUA, E. JOSI, E. KIRSCHBAUM, *Esplorazioni sotto la Confessione di san Pietro in Vaticano, eseguite negli anni 1940-1949,* Vols. I-II, Vatican City 1951.

JOCELYN TOYNBEE AND J. B. WARD PERKINS, *The Shrine of St. Peter and the Vatican Excavations,* Pantheon Books, New York, 1956.

A. PRANDI, *La zona archeologica della Confessio Vaticana. I monumenti del II secolo,* Vatican City 1957.

E. KIRSCHBAUM, *Die Gräber der Apostelfürsten,* Frankfurt on Main, 1957.

——— *The Tomb of SS. Peter and Paul,* St. Martin's Press, New York, 1959.

V. THE TESTIMONY OF THE INSCRIPTIONS

M. GUARDUCCI, *Cristo e san Pietro in un documento precostantiniano della necropoli vaticana,* Rome 1953.

——— *I graffiti sotto la Confessione di san Pietro in Vaticano,* Vols. I-III, Vatican City 1958.

VI. THE CULT OF THE APOSTLES PETER AND PAUL ON THE
APPIAN WAY

P. STYGER, *Il monumento apostolico della via Appia,* in "Dissertazioni della Pontificia Accademia romana di archeologia," 1918, pp. 1-115.

R. LANCIANI, *La "Memoria Apostolorum" al III miglio dell'Appia e gli scavi di S. Sebastiano,* in "Dissertazioni della Pontificia Accademia romana di archeologia," 1920, pp. 55-111.

H. LIETZMANN, *Petrus und Paulus in Rom,* second edition, Berlin-Leipzig 1927, pp. 145-169.

F. TOLOTTI, *Memorie degli Apostoli in Catacumbas: rilievo critico della Basilica Apostolorum al III miglio della via Appia* (No. XIX in the collection "Amici delle Catacombe") Rome 1953.

M. GUARDUCCI, *Due presunte date consolari a S. Sebastiano,* in "Rendiconti della Pontificia Accademia romana di archeologia," Vol. XXVIII (1955-56), pp. 181-195.

J. RUYSSCHAERT, *Les documents littéraires de la double tradition romaine des tombes apostoliques,* in "Revue d'histoire ecclésiastique," Vol. III (1957), pp. 791-831.

The vast bibliography related to the excavations under St. Peter's Basilica has been assembled with exemplary diligence, for the years 1941-1958, by J. RUYSSCHAERT, *Recherches et études autour de la Confession de la Basilique Vaticane (1940-1958). État de la question et bibliographie,* in *Triplice omaggio a Sua Santita Pio XII,* Vatican City 1958, Vol. II, pp. 33-47.

In quotations from Christian authors I have referred only to texts in the *Patrologia Latina* or the *Patrologia Graeca,* and in citing epigraphs I have referred only to the *Corpus Inscriptionum Latinarum.*

INDEX

(Prepared by Joseph McLellan)

192

In references to Tacitus, Pliny, Martial and other classical Latin and Greek authors, I have used the sectional numbers found in all standard editions, rather than page numbers referring to any specific edition.

THE AUTHOR AND HER BOOK

MARGHERITA GUARDUCCI, *author, and professor of Greek epig-raphy, was born in Florence, Italy, December 20, 1902. She received her doctorate in Greek literature from the Univer-sity of Bologna. Her studies were completed at the Archaeology schools of Rome and Athens. At this point she began to specialize in epigraphy. In 1942 the University of Rome ap-pointed her to the Chair of Greek Epigraphy. She is the author of 160 monographs on ancient history, archaeology and epigraphy, published in academic journals and reviews. Her monographs illuminate the various aspects of ancient Greek and Roman civilizations. Much of her work is based on archaeological explorations of the island of Crete and involves its history and antiquity, which she incorporated in a vo-luminous work entitled* Inscriptiones Creticae, *which re-vealed the meanings of the Greek and Roman inscriptions found there. This work has been of key importance to all scholars of antiquity. Since 1952 Doctor Guarducci has been at work on her interpretation of the inscriptions found under the basilica of St. Peter's in Rome.* THE TOMB OF ST. PETER *is her own popularization of this dramatic investi-gation, which appeared in Rome in 1958 in three massive* volumes under the title of I graffiti sotto la Confessione di san Pietro in Vaticano. *She is a member of the* Pontificia Accademia di Archeologia, *the* Accademia Nazionale dei Lincei, *and the* Accademia di Scienze e Lettere di Napoli and the Instituto di Studi Romani. *She is the author of* Cristo e san Pietro in un documento preconstantiniano della necropoli vaticana *and* of La Tomba di Pietro.

THE TOMB OF ST. PETER *(Hawthorn, 1960) was designed by Sidney Feinberg and completely manufactured by American Book-Stratford Press, Inc. The body type was set on the Linotype in Baskerville, a modern reproduction of the types cut in 1760 by John Baskerville, of Birmingham, England, reflecting the style of stone inscriptions.*

A HAWTHORN BOOK